Also by Mor

## Nonfiction

*Social Change and Scientific Organization*

TRILOGY ON HUMAN CONSCIOUSNESS:
*The Reenchantment of the World*
*Coming to Our Senses*
*Wandering God: A Study in Nomadic Spirituality*

TRILOGY ON THE AMERICAN EMPIRE:
*The Twilight of American Culture*
*Dark Ages America: The Final Phase of Empire*
*Why America Failed: The Roots of Imperial Decline*

*Neurotic Beauty: An Outsider Looks at Japan*
*Genio: The Story of Italian Genius*
*Eminent Post-Victorians*
*Healing: The Defining Root of Our Existence*
*The Soul of Russia*
*The Crisis of Our Time*
*Soul-Changers*
*The Jews and the Irrational*

# Memoir

*Spinning Straw Into Gold*

# Essays

*A Question of Values*

*Are We There Yet?*

# Poetry

*Counting Blessings*

# Fiction

*Destiny*

*The Man Without Qualities*

*The Heart of the Matter*

*Reaching for Utopia*

*They Took Him Away in a Wagon*

*Empire's End*

*The Doll*

*The Girl in the Café*

# AGAINST CIVILIZATION

## THE ANTHROPOLOGICAL CRITIQUE OF MODERNITY

### MORRIS BERMAN

© Morris Berman, 2025

All rights reserved.

ISBN: 9798275373868

Cover art: *Hand Paintings at the Cave of Hands in Patagonia, Argentina, 11,000-7,000 B.C.*, R.M. Nunes via iStock.

Cover design and interior layout by Jeffrey P. Fisher

Author photo by John Trotter

Who are we and where are we going? Why are we, with all our "progress," so limited in understanding & sympathy & the ability to give each other real freedom? Why with our emphasis on the individual are we still so blinded by the urge to conform?...The world—and really I mean the West—has no interest in change or self-improvement...
—Lily King, *Euphoria*, spoken by "Nell," her Margaret Mead character

A well-ordered humanism does not begin with itself, but puts things back in their place. It puts the world before life, life before man, and the respect of others before love of self. This is the lesson that the people we call "savages" teach us: a lesson of modesty, decency and discretion in the face of a world that preceded our species and that will survive it.
—Claude Lévi-Strauss, 1972 interview

A tribe which eats roots and spiders and wears no clothes may have solved complex problems of social organization far more satisfactorily than we have.
—Sanche de Gramont, "There Are No Superior Societies," *New York Times Magazine*, 28 January 1968

## Contents

Preface: The Girl from Utah ix
Introduction xv

1. Lucien Lévy-Bruhl 1
2. Franz Boas 5
3. Alfred Kroeber 11
4. Ruth Benedict 23
5. Margaret Mead 35
6. Gregory Bateson 45
7. Zora Neale Hurston 65
8. Claude Lévi-Strauss 75
9. Marshall Sahlins 83
10. Pierre Clastres 95

Epilogue: Great Lives 103
Notes 107
About the Author 119

## Preface: The Girl from Utah

During the spring semester of 1997, I was a visiting professor at Weber State University in Ogden, Utah. In the course of living there for a few months, I met a woman who was about ten years younger than myself, and somehow, we became friends. "Angela" (not her real name) was married to a construction worker; our friendship was purely Platonic in nature. But for some reason, we got together fairly often, and always had a lot to talk about. Angie had gotten a bachelor's degree in urban anthropology from some university—I forget which—and her thesis was based on research she had done in some African metropolis; I think it was Nairobi. It was an analysis of the mythology of that city; the dominant (and largely invisible) beliefs that kept the city, if not the entire country, functioning.

She had chosen, she told me, not to go on to graduate study in the field. Instead—oddly enough—she pursued a career in computers, specifically, large mainframe IBM

## Preface: The Girl from Utah

types that were then in use in various institutions, such as hospitals. She trained as a troubleshooter, being called upon as "Ms. Fixit" when something went wrong. The only time she thought about anthropology, she told me, was when the two of us got together. No one else was interested, her husband included, and for the most part, neither was she.

"I don't get it," I confessed. "Exactly how did this career switch occur?" What she said was that she understood that the methodology she had learned to apply to Africa could easily be applied to America, which had a very different mythology—the American Dream and all that—but was still, nevertheless, a mythology.

"I saw through America," she went on; "it's not very difficult to do, if you've had even a slight amount of anthropological training. Which left me at a crossroads. The choice was to live within the mythology—which is what 99 percent of Americans are doing—or to live outside of it, analyze it, and write about it. It was clear to me that the latter path, the path of the anthropologist, was a hard slog. The anthropological gaze, so to speak, is characterized by distancing. You are more or less isolated, swimming against the current. So I deliberately shut that door, as an act of will, and opted for the standard American life. And the fact is that I'm OK with it."

"How can you be OK with it?" I replied, trying not to raise my voice. "I mean, for the 99 percent, it works fine, because they don't know any other way of life. They are just breathing nitrogen, so to speak. But you *do* know; you've inhaled oxygen, which is why we are able to have this very

## Preface: The Girl from Utah

conversation. How do you manage to live inside of a dual consciousness—which is what it is?" Angela put her hand on my shoulder.

"I'm telling you, Maury; it's not that hard. Like I told you before, you are literally the one person with whom I can talk to about this. And in two or three months, you'll be gone, and the anthro part of me will shut down once again. Please don't think I'm suffering, because I don't regret my decision. I have my life with Bob, I have a job I find more or less interesting, and I have something of a social life as well. If my anthro life functions as a shadow, it's a pretty faint shadow, by now, and one that I don't really miss."

"I still can't get my mind around this," I told her. "The anthropological perspective is a profound insight into the nature of society, culture, human life. Can one really turn it off like a faucet? Angie, until I met you, I never knew such a thing was even possible."

"Well, it is, and I can; turn it off, that is."

I need to tell you, the reader, that this is a true story. I've embellished it about 10 percent, for narrative smoothness, but Angela did exist, and this is a factual description of what she had done, and how she was living in the present time. Reflecting on it nearly thirty years later, I'm still a bit amazed by it.

Let's shift gears for a moment. Angela didn't want to live as an outlier, an outsider, someone with a unique (if fairly accurate) perspective on life. It struck her as being a painful path, and I'm not sure she was wrong. But this raises the question, at least for me, as to why *anyone* would want to be an anthropologist. As Aristotle pointed out, we are social animals, by nature; the Greek word for a private person who removed himself from the larger society was *idiōtēs*. You can take it from there.

So what, then, are the motives behind this choice of career? Let me speculate on this.

-Deep intellectual curiosity, specifically, wanting to know what it means to be human

-A fascination with otherness, with the exotic, with peoples radically different from ourselves

-"Mirroring": the notion that by learning about the Other, we actually come to know ourselves; and beyond that, that this can lead to a rejection of the notion of Western superiority, to the point that the observed culture may start to look superior to our own

-The belief that "primitive" cultures reveal man in his "true," "unadulterated" state, i.e. without the influence (or corruption) of civilization; the theory that the so-called primitive is the real, the genuine, human condition

-Being an outlier by nature, perhaps from a very early age; having a contrarian personality; resonating to the remark made by the French anthropologist Pierre Clastres, that the thought which is the most profound is the one that moves against the grain.

There may, of course, be other motives at play; I'm just listing the ones that most readily come to mind. But this business of "nitrogen vs. oxygen" that I mentioned above, and the consequences of choosing one as opposed to the other, was captured centuries ago in a Sufi tale, updated in modern times by the British writer Doris Lessing in *Briefing for a Descent into Hell*. Roughly, the story goes like this: there is a heavenly abode inhabited by an enlightened race, and one member of this society wants to go down to Earth, live among the earthlings, and experience what their life is like. Before he leaves, one of the elders outfits him with a supply of water native to their culture, telling him that he should drink only this water, and avoid the Earth water at all costs, which, he says, will drive him insane.

So the man descends, and mingles with the earthlings. It is very confusing, because as far as he can make out, everything they say is nonsense. He simply can't understand them, and is unable to make any friends, or be part of this society. He is completely alienated, isolated. Meanwhile, as time goes by his supply of heavenly water continues to shrink, until it finally runs out. He manages to hold out for a while, not drink the earthly water, but finally, on the verge of dying of thirst, he gives in, and drinks what everyone else drinks. And suddenly, all that had been "nonsense" makes perfect sense to him. He engages in conversations, makes friends, has no trouble fitting into earthly society. He is, at last, part of the crowd. He is "happy" now; his former life is but a dim memory.

I guess one might say that something like this happened to my friend Angela. As for me, I miss our conversations.

# INTRODUCTION
## CULTURAL RELATIVISM AND THE REFLECTION IN THE MIRROR

> Mythic culture is not a subset of theoretic culture, nor will it ever be. It is older than theoretic culture and remains to this day an indispensable way of relating to the world.
>
> —Robert Bellah, "What is Axial about the Axial Age?"

The anthropological critique of civilization, and of modern society, is rooted in the notions of cultural relativism and a backfire or boomerang effect, whereupon the researcher is confronted with the possibility that the society he or she is studying might actually be superior to their own. Cultural relativism facilitates this possibility by asserting that we can only understand a culture on its own terms, rather than on the terms of another culture (namely, our own). To take a rather pointed example of this, Shahid Bolsen, a controversial Muslim intellectual, has called into question the Western use of the word "underdeveloped." It is a term that the West likes to apply to those countries that lag

## INTRODUCTION

behind the West in terms of economic and technological expansion and industrial growth, which are seen as the purpose of life. But these, Bolsen argues, are not the only possible yardsticks, or criteria, of development. The West, he tells us, is underdeveloped in terms of morality, spirituality, ethics, equality, sustainability, community, and so on. It seems hard to argue with this. Arthur Koestler raised precisely the same issue more than sixty years ago, pointing out that the first type of development had raced ahead of the second type, much to the detriment of America and Europe. Like Bolsen, he regarded this as a very unhealthy situation for the West.(1)

In this study, I want to examine the work of those anthropologists who have made major contributions to the concepts of cultural relativism and "reverse superiority." With one exception—putting Zora Neale Hurston after Gregory Bateson—I'm going to do this in chronological order, by year of birth, starting and ending with two French scholars, Lucien Lévy-Bruhl (b. 1857) and Pierre Clastres (b. 1934). My justification for the exception is that Benedict, Mead, and Bateson form a "trio," and belong in a cluster. Benedict and Mead had a very deep intellectual and romantic relationship; Mead and Bateson had something similar (in fact were married for fourteen years). In between the two Frenchmen, we shall meet a number of others who lent their particular expertise to the subject at hand. The result has been a body of work that many regard as irrefutable, and which, of course, the West has completely ignored in terms of self-transparency—a choice that, if we are going to be candid, very likely constitutes a major factor in its decline. It calls to mind the Book

## INTRODUCTION

of Daniel (5:25-31), where the famous handwriting on the wall predicted the end of the Babylonian kingdom of Belshazzar. Did they heed the warning? Take a wild guess.

I need to preface this discussion, however, with a brief foray into the work of the sociologist Robert Bellah, and the psychologist Merlin Donald, regarding the evolution of human mental capacities.(2) According to Donald, the human race went from a Mimetic stage, to a Mythic stage, to a Theoretic one. Mimesis consists of imitation and repetition, and is the basis of crafts, dance, music, and tool use, and goes back 4 million years. The Mythic stage is about narrative—speech and storytelling—and goes back about 400,000 years. And finally, the Theoretic stage, which is relatively recent, is where we are now, consisting of critical thinking, writing, analysis, and reflection. The crucial point, says Donald, is that these stages don't replace one another; rather, they just accumulate. The modern mind is in fact a mixture of all three. After all, we still dance and sing, and we still tell stories, i.e., generate myths and narratives (including secular ones). And if analytic thinking can do things that the other two modes can't, he says, it is nevertheless the case that these latter modes are "extremely subtle and powerful ways of thinking. They cannot be matched by analytic thought for intuitive speed, complexity, and shrewdness." Hence the epigraph to this Introduction, by Robert Bellah, suggesting that properly understood, the Mythic mindset is superior to the Theoretic one; or at the very least, that the latter is seriously incomplete. Both Bellah and Donald argue that we simply cannot live without these earlier stages; that they are intrinsic to what it is to be human. In fact, they are hardwired into the human brain, whereas the Theoretic way of thinking is not. This is a reality that all of the anthropologists in this study had to contend with.

One final word: This study makes no attempt at a comprehensive analysis of any of the individuals involved. The bibliographies of such analyses, not to mention (in most cases) the works of these individuals, would fill a warehouse. In addition, although I did do extensive research in the anthropological literature some years ago, and wrote a book on the subject (*Wandering God*), I never had any formal training in anthropology and cannot claim to be anything other than a student of the subject (even if a dedicated one). As a result, what I am offering here are cameos, not comprehensive studies. The latter have been executed (or attempted) by numerous scholars far more equipped to do so than I. My focus is elsewhere: to offer glimpses, or to capture the essences, of the individuals involved; what I believe is their particular or noteworthy contributions to anthropology, and perhaps, in the long run, *inshallah*, to society at large.

## Chapter 1

## Lucien Lévy-Bruhl

[Lévy-Bruhl says that] mystical thought responds to a need in human nature, for rational knowledge cannot be fully satisfying. It separates the subject from its object too much. For example, the notion of God which it can construct does not replace the feeling of participation in the divine.

—Jean Cazeneuve, *Lucien Lévy-Bruhl*

The primitive, he argued, is not a bad scientist; he is a good mystic; and the intellectual procedures of the primitive mind are not deficient applications of the rules of logic and science—they are alogical not illogical, nonrational not irrational.

—Richard Shweder, "Anthropology's romantic rebellion against the enlightenment, or there's more to thinking than reason and evidence"

Now it turns out that a number of anthropologists were onto these ideas long before Donald and Bellah appeared on the scene. Outstanding among them was Lucien Lévy-Bruhl (1857-1939), whose scholarly influence was enormous, even though he was an "armchair anthropologist"—he never did any actual fieldwork. However, he had access to a large literature of ethnographic studies, missionary reports, and travelers' accounts, and put them to good use. In the course of his career he held a chair at the Sorbonne, was a visiting professor at Harvard, lectured at the Johns Hopkins University as well as UC Berkeley. He wrote numerous books on the "primitive" mind, which he regarded favorably, and in no way inferior to the Western scientific mind. (E.g., *Ethics and Moral Science, How Natives Think, Primitive Mentality*.) This was his cultural relativism, that one had to evaluate a society from the inside, on its own terms—what is called in anthropology an "emic" perspective, as opposed to an exterior, or "etic" one, in which the observed society is (usually) judged by Western standards, and typically found wanting. There was, he asserted, no such thing as a universal human nature, and no way of establishing a hierarchy between the customs of "primitive" societies and those of modern ones. This enabled him to cast doubt on the Eurocentric worldview.(1)

Lévy-Bruhl's key concept was "participation," which he posited in contrast to Aristotelian logic, specifically the rule of non-contradiction (a thing could not be and not-be at the same time). Within the primitive mode of perception and behavior, a thing could be both singular and plural, both itself and something else, and both here and elsewhere at the same time. So the world was divided into two mindsets, the primitive and the civilized. But the modern or Western belief that the former mindset was incoherent was deeply misguided; it was just a different type of coherence from the Aristotelian one. Not inferior reasoning, in other words, just different reasoning. Dreams, omens, divination, hallucinations, and the supernatural were all part of this mental system. In a word, he argued, human beings have a mystical, creative side that transcends the logic of rational thought. The anthropologist Richard Shweder rightly regarded him as "the founding father of romanticism" within the field of cognitive anthropology.(2)

In addition, Jean Cazeneuve, his biographer, writes that primitive man does not have a notion of a separate self. "He does not see himself as a creature distinct from all beings and things which surround him...There is, therefore...a kinship of essence between all things, animate or inanimate. The spiritual is not distinct from the material." (In contemporary terms, this is often referred to as "the kinship worldview.") Nothing is absurd to primitive man, Cazeneuve goes on to say:

> The mythical world is characterized by fluidity of images and by metamorphoses. Everything is possible in that world; categories there are not separate so that beings can be at one and the same time human and animal. For primitive man this constitutes reality *par excellence*, at one and the same time prenatural and supernatural.

As a side note, I need to say that I discovered precisely this worldview in my study of Russian literature, which included Pushkin, Gogol, Andrei Bely, and Mikhail

Bulgakov (*The Master and Margarita*). All of these writers violated normal reality in major ways, their source for this being the primitive mentality of the Russian peasant-shamanic tradition. Perhaps Gogol said it best in his surreal short story, "The Nose": "Perfect nonsense goes on in the world. Sometimes there is no plausibility at all."(3)

But is it really nonsense? The year before he died, Lévy-Bruhl wrote that if you want to understand the thinking of so-called primitive peoples, you have to get inside their heads, "and through an effort of empathy with them undergo their mystical experience." In his final years, he modified his views somewhat, allowing for a spectrum of intermediate states. The "mystical mentality," he wrote, "is present in every human mind"—an assertion that has been validated independently by research in cognitive psychology. It's just a question of degree, which varies from society to society—including our own.

Yet somehow, the primitive-civilized dichotomy remained Lévy-Bruhl's fundamental outlook, and although, to my knowledge, he never said so explicitly, his position seemed to be that it was we who were lacking, not the natives. I believe Merlin Donald and Robert Bellah were saying much the same thing.

## Chapter 2

# Franz Boas

[I am confident that anthropological discoveries] will teach us to tolerate to a greater extent other forms of civilization than our own.

—Franz Boas, *The Mind of Primitive Man*

I had seen that they enjoyed life, and a hard life, as we do; that nature is also beautiful to them; that feelings of friendship also root in the Eskimo heart; that, although the character of their life is so rude compared to civilized life, the Eskimo is a man as we are; that his feelings, his virtues, and his shortcomings are based in human nature, like ours.

—Franz Boas, concluding words of his essay, "A Year among the Eskimo"

Franz Boas (1858-1942) is known as the "father of American anthropology," in particular, for promoting the idea of cultural relativism, a phrase that he himself coined.(1)

Cultural relativism (CR) ran counter to the social evolutionary theory of the day, which saw human beings developing from a "primitive" state to that of a "civilized" one, the latter represented by the contemporary white European—an outlook known as ethnocentrism. Before we review his life and work, it will be helpful to delineate what CR actually means.

In a nutshell, CR is the principle that an individual's beliefs, values, and practices should be understood within the context of his or her own culture, rather than being judged by the standards of another culture (typically, our own). It argues that there is no universal standard of right and wrong; what is considered "normal" in one culture might be regarded as immoral or repugnant in another culture. For example, Mexicans eat insects; it is part of an old culinary tradition, whereas most Americans find this distasteful, or worse. More dramatically, female circumcision is practiced in thirty countries in Africa, the Middle East, and Asia, while most nations of the world condemn it as a violation of human rights. While CR argues for tolerance, understanding, and non-judgmentalism, the latter example suggests that it also has a potentially down side.

Less controversial are things such as arranged marriages vs. ones based on romantic love and individual choice; a difference, perhaps, between East and West. This conflict is quite brilliantly, and sympathetically, illustrated, for example, in the film *Learning to Drive*, starring Ben Kingsley and Patricia Clarkson. By the end of the story it becomes hard to decide which of the two options is better, inasmuch as both are seen to have serious disadvantages.

But in the discipline of anthropology, CR means studying and understanding cultures on their own terms. All of the world's peoples, said Boas, had created unique cultures, ones that were complex and beautiful, hardly stages on the way to becoming "civilized." As a result, he concluded, there are no superior cultures—something that Claude Lévi-Strauss would argue his entire life (see Chapter 8). In fact, primitive art and languages were in many cases more complex and sophisticated than their Western counterparts. There were no universal criteria of evaluation; one could not say that some cultures were more valuable than others. The Western desire to do this, he asserted, was the result of ethnocentrism, not objectivity. This, among other things, was Boas' great legacy—a legacy that lies at the heart of American anthropology to this day. In the course of his professorship at Columbia University, 1899-1942, Boas mentored Alfred Kroeber, Edward Sapir, Ruth Benedict, Margaret Mead, Zora Neale Hurston, Stanley Diamond, and Robert Lowie, among others—scholars who became leaders in the field, some of them famous beyond the field (books by Benedict and Mead sold in the millions). Although Lévi-Strauss was never a student of his, he was significantly influenced by his work. In 1942, at a luncheon at the Columbia University Faculty Club, Boas had a stroke and died in Lévi-Strauss' arms. There is something symbolic in that, it seems to me.

Boas' fieldwork, and his commitment to empirical evidence, are legendary. Reading over biographical profiles of the man, one wonders how a single individual had the energy to accomplish what he did. Boas spent a year alone with the Inuit of Baffin Island (1883-84), and also carried out expeditions to northern and western Canada. During his stay with the Inuit (a word that means "the people"), he traveled to other local groups, covering 5,000 kilometers. He visited the tribes between Vancouver Island and the mainland—all seventy of them(!!). At one point he did a trek of twenty-five hours with an Inuit guide, in the freezing cold. He would later refer to his year with the Inuit as *herzensbildung*—education of the heart, i.e., emotional awareness. He saw that there was no understanding without empathy, i.e., without getting inside of a culture. And in addition, that it was only through a study of the Other that one could begin to understand one's own culture, one's Self. If you relativize your own culture, he wrote, you can then understand other cultures, and vice versa.

Boas also studied the Kwakiutl people—this for forty years—even including their dance practice (focusing on their approach to rhythm, and its related emotions), and wrote several books about their language and way of life. Their language, and the languages of a whole number of tribes in British Columbia, are very complex; he mastered all of them (the Salish, the Kootenay, the Bella Coola, etc.). In 1896, he offered a course on native languages, which he taught out of his apartment in Greenwich Village. He also studied the folklore and art of these tribes. At one point in the 1880s, the Kwakiutl invited him to a potlach ceremony, the lone white man there, and honored him by calling him a "chief." One of his books, published in 1895, was *The Social Organization and the Secret Societies of the Kwakiutl Indians*.

Boas argued with Lucien Lévy-Bruhl over the issue of the primitive mind. As we saw, Lévy-Bruhl believed in a radical split between the primitive mentality and our own, although he modified this somewhat toward the end of his life. Boas held that this dichotomy was spurious, that belief systems that privileged "magical" thinking could emerge in any culture, and that therefore there was no difference between the mind of primitive people and civilized ones. This was a theme he repeated over and over again. In a lecture he gave at Columbia in 1907, he stated that one had to "guard against the inference that divergence from the European type is synonymous with inferiority." His most famous work is probably *The Mind of Primitive Man* (1911).

One begins to wonder if Boas was real. His fieldwork, his publications, his travels, his teaching and mentoring, his university administration—no other anthropologist in the history of the discipline comes close to this achievement, at least in terms of sheer quantity, which comes across as practically supernatural. During his life, he did the work of ten people, maybe more. He sounds like a figure from a science fiction novel. And yet he existed, and he did all of the above, and in so doing, he dramatically altered the perceptual landscape. In her obituary of Boas in *The Nation*, shortly after his death, Ruth Benedict put it this way: "At eighty-four he had not sold out, or stultified himself, or locked himself in a dogmatic cage." What's that line from the bible? "There were giants on the earth in those days." Franz Boas was a giant, nothing less.

## Chapter 3

## Alfred Kroeber

[Our expedition found traces in the artifacts of] the smallest and and most remarkable people, the last free survivors of the American red man, who by an unexampled fortitude and stubbornness of character have succeeded in holding out against the overwhelming tide of civilization twenty-five years longer even than Geronimo.

—Alfred Kroeber, "The Elusive Mill Creeks" (1911)

It is but just that I should mention the circumstances which raised the hand of the Mill Creeks against the whites. As in almost every similar instance in American History, the first act of injustice, the first spilling of blood, must be laid at the white man's door.

—Robert Anderson, *Fighting the Mill Creeks* (1909)

Alfred Kroeber (1876-1960): a great anthropologist in the Boas mold, being Boas' first doctoral student. Father of one of America's outstanding writers, Ursula Le Guin, whose science fiction—in reality, commentaries on the destructiveness of modern life—is very anthropological in nature. Like Boas, Kroeber was a workhorse, author of the *Handbook of the Indians of California* (1925), containing 1,000 pages of ethnographic data. And then there was his extensive fieldwork among the Arapaho of the Great Plains. His textbook, *Anthropology*, was widely used in universities for many years. He was the first professor appointed to the Department of Anthropology at UC Berkeley, and was curator and director of its Museum of Anthropology from 1909 to 1946, when he retired after a lifetime of achievement. Down to 2020, the Department of Anthropology on the Berkeley campus was located in Kroeber Hall.(1)

That being said, Alfred Kroeber is essentially known today for one particular thing: his close friendship with, and protection of, the last living member of the Yahi tribe, a man named "Ishi" (which means "man" in the Yana language; no one ever found out his real name), who was discovered outside Oroville, California, in 1911, and who died of tuberculosis in 1916. Kroeber's first wife, Henriette, died of the same disease less than three years earlier, and Theodora, his second wife, wrote up the story of Ishi in *Ishi in Two Worlds*, a book that sold half a million copies within fifteen years of its publication in 1961. The story was also the subject of a 1992 film, *The Last of His Tribe*, starring Jon Voight (as Kroeber) and Graham Greene—an Oneida Indian and Canadian actor, not to be confused with the famous British author—as Ishi. (Actually, there were several films and documentaries about Ishi, both before and after 1992.)

The Yahi people, a subgroup of the Yana, was an indigenous community decimated by invasion and genocide at the hands of white settlers during the California Gold Rush, which kicked off in 1848. In fact, they had been living in that region for several thousand years before the arrival of the white man. The massacre of Native Americans in California preceded this, however; prior to that arrival, the native population has been estimated at 310,000; by 1920, the figure had dropped to 6,400.

After he was discovered, Ishi was taken to the Museum of Anthropology in San Francisco by Kroeber and another anthropologist, Thomas Waterman, where he was given a place to live, and eventually the job of janitor at a salary of $25 per month. At the Museum, he would do weekly public displays, e.g. stringing a bow, making fire, or fashioning a chipped arrowhead, which he would then give to someone in the audience, whose number often exceeded a thousand individuals in a single afternoon. In addition to crafting tools and weapons, he was often taken hunting; something he was very skilled at. Theodora wrote of his time there:

> Ishi's "public" was a serious minded and a devoted one… [such] that when Ishi fashioned a tool or weapon under their eyes, or made fire with his primitive fire drill, they were seeing in actuality the reenactment of man's oldest and fundamental skills…Watching Ishi at work, the long road of history, lost in the darkness of remoteness, became illuminated and its distances telescoped, for man is the world's craftsman…

As Theodora tells it, the story of Ishi is an incredible one; it sounds like it could be a fairy tale, except that it really happened. From one perspective, it is a triumphant story, even a heroic one; from another, it would seem to be sad, and very moving. This latter aspect is poignantly captured in the 1992 film, which I'll discuss below.

As soon as the existence of Ishi was made public, Americans went nuts over him. He became a hero to Californians, a man of myth and mystery. Photos of him were purchased as treasured mementos. Women sent him food and clothing; people wanted to learn everything about him. Letters to the Museum expressed concern that he be cared for, and happy. "Ishi's human appeal," wrote Theodora, "seems to have been a universal one." Many, she adds, saw him in the mold of Rousseau's noble savage.

All of this raises an interesting question: What was going on here? What was the psychology of all this, that Ishi could generate such excitement? We can never know for sure, but my own guess is something like this: in Jungian terms, Ishi was a "shadow" figure for civilization. He was everything Americans were not, but perhaps secretly wanted to be. In general, said Theodora, California Indians were reserved, contemplative, and philosophical. They would have looked askance at self-promotion, boasting, and aggressive behavior. Their ideal was the man of restraint, of dignity, and Ishi epitomized that ideal. He was averse to any sort of exhibitionism, display, or attempts to demonstrate one's skill; averse to the white man's competitiveness, the (tedious) desire to always be first. In contrast, what made Ishi happy was to be able to *give* something to someone: arrowheads, spear points, even a bow which had taken him many hours to make. Kroeber said he was the most patient man he ever knew; that he radiated a deep sense of contentment. Very few Americans, or Westerners in general, fit that description; in fact, pretty much the opposite is true. (See Epilogue, below.) After Ishi died, his friend and physician, Saxton Pope, wrote: "He looked upon us as sophisticated children —smart, but not wise." This could have been his epitaph, but it strikes me as being America's epitaph as well, minus the sophistication. (Well, American history would suggest that we're also not particularly smart, it seems to me. Which doesn't leave us a whole lot to admire, unfortunately.)

In an essay he wrote in 1920, "The Medical History of Ishi," Pope asserted his belief that the people who came to look at Ishi were looking for something in him, in particular, traits such as compassion for others, disgust with modern civilization (which Ishi did not, in fact, possess), and a desire to be wild. Lost parts of themselves, we might say. Ishi was, in effect, a mirror, or alter ego, but even more, an alternative mode of being in the world.

Additional support for the Jungian approach can be found in poems that appeared in local newspapers, such as the *Examiner* and the *Bulletin*, shortly after Ishi's arrival in San Francisco. They poked fun at modern life, and warned Ishi to resist its lure. They were often pretty blunt. For example:

> Happy old Ishi!
> Free from all anxiety!
> Bless your stars you weren't born
> In civilized society!

Some Californians, writes Douglas Cazaux Sackman (in *Wild Men*), worried that all their possessions "didn't make them better than the man who had none of them" (as Sitting Bull famously observed in 1877). He quotes from a poem, "Cave Man, Beware," by Ernest Hopkins, which appeared in the *San Francisco Bulletin*, also shortly after Ishi was discovered. Hopkins begins by asking what Ishi thought of "our speed and land train...of our houses and churches and clothes, cramped and unaired and confined." He continues:

> Collars and manners and fuss:
> Let us "improve" you and iron you out
> train you to flirt and to cuss
> Come let us aid you, but sonny, by 'Gee,
> What if you've got it on us?

What indeed.

In any case, let's return to Theodora's book. It provides a detailed portrait of who Ishi was, and an account of his relatively short life in San Francisco. Although shy and introverted, Ishi was also quite sociable. In his time in the city, he made three very close (white) friends. The first was Thomas Waterman, an anthropologist, who had fetched him from Oroville and brought him to Alfred Kroeber in 1911. Waterman spoke a broken Yana, which helped. He brought Ishi to his classes at UC Berkeley, where Ishi demonstrated making fire to his fascinated students. As Ishi neared death, in 1916, Waterman wrote to Kroeber (the italics are his): "*He was the best friend I had in the world.*" Not the best Native American friend—no. The best friend, period.

Kroeber was, of course, his second friend. It was he who shepherded Ishi's public appearances, preventing the merely curious from getting to him. The relationship they had was one of respect and trust. Ishi saw that Kroeber understood him; that he knew something about the Yana worldview. Finally, there was Saxton Pope, already referred to. Pope spoke some Yana, studied archery with Ishi, and spent many hours with him. Pope's hospital was next door to the Museum, and Ishi visited it often. He would, like a physician, make the rounds(!). He was quiet and affable (although he occasionally sang), and made the patients feel good. He was also drawn into the various games of the interns, med students, and orderlies. He watched Pope operate many times, and regarded him as a great healer, or *kuwi*. By 1914 he had an English vocabulary of 500 or 600 words, and proved to be something of a storyteller. Pope later recalled that at one point Ishi told him forty distinct tales, drawn from the body of oral literature and myth of the Yana people.

According to Sackman, Ishi especially "lit up" around children. He would play games with them, and in two cases he carved out wooden dolls for each of them. A girl named Dorothy Stevens was ten years old when she met him at the Museum, and years later commented, "I thought him one of the nicest men I ever met." Ishi possessed some undefinable quality that attracted everyone, of every age.

Ishi's adaptability to civilization was remarkable. He managed to go from Stone Age to Steel Age practically overnight. "He speedily assimilated civilized ways," wrote Kroeber. He enjoyed riding the streetcars of San Francisco, and was a frequent consumer of various items at a row of shops on Seventh Avenue between Golden Gate Park and Judah Street. Everyone greeted him: grocer, baker, tobacconist, cobbler. Plus, he had no resistance to the conveniences of modern life, including tables, chairs, beds, running water, electricity, matches, and glue, which he now used in his craftwork. And whereas most indigenous people in California were wary of whites (with obvious reason), Ishi was trusting toward them, even friendly. He did become something of a legend, as a result of all this.

As for Kroeber, he was devastated by Ishi's death, and it took him several years to recover from it. Jack Glazier, in his review of several films about Ishi, writes that "Ishi's death had plunged Kroeber into a deep professional questioning compounded by self-doubt." Why would that be the case? Just my own take, but it seems to me that Ishi was, for Kroeber, a lifeline to wholeness, in particular to the emotional side of life that Kroeber as a scientist had largely ignored, or even repressed; and when he died, Kroeber was cast adrift—a lost soul. He took a leave of absence from his teaching duties at Berkeley in order to become a psychoanalyst, and work through the whole relationship, not to mention the meaning of his life. He confessed that he was overwhelmed by a feeling of *sturm und drang* (storm and stress). Recovery was, indeed, a slow and even tortuous process.

But his second marriage, to Theodora, did a lot to make him feel whole again, as did continued contact with the Native Americans of California, and pouring his heart out in letters to his colleague-in-arms, the linguist and anthropologist Edward Sapir. In retrospect, one thing becomes clear: Ishi was the central reality of Alfred Kroeber's life. Certainly, as an anthropologist, he accomplished a tremendous amount, in terms of fieldwork, teaching, publications, and museum administration. But he will always be remembered, and rightly so, as the man who befriended Ishi, and took care of him. Ultimately, Ishi became Kroeber's alter ego.

And even then, there is a larger issue here, one that goes beyond the relationship of two individuals, and was pointedly captured by Douglas Sackman in his Afterword to *Wild Men*. He writes:

> Ishi was and continues to be so fascinating in large part because his story seemed to represent an alternative to the modern world. And although certainly Ishi was partially a screen on which to project such colonial nostalgia, the truth is that Ishi, and many other Native Americans, did offer an alternative. They had another bundle of stories to tell, ones that countered modernity and its metanarrative of progress.

This was also the real theme of the 1992 movie, cited above, which is more than just about Ishi. It is, in fact, a very moving film. It depicts, quite explicitly, the brutality of the white man, wantonly massacring innocent, defenseless people, and it does a good job of showing the callousness of the white Western world in general, largely cut off from all sources of emotion and spirituality. And this also applies to Kroeber, as the film (says Jack Glazier) exposes his clinical, fact-based view of anthropology, leaving no room for emotional truths. To wit: Kroeber was in New York when Ishi died, in 1916. He had taken a sabbatical, traveling around to various cities. He knew Ishi was ill, but didn't return to California, because he was in a hurry to finish his book, *Handbook of Indians of California*. His colleague Edward Gifford wrote to him about Ishi's impending death, but he chose to stay in New York. He tried to prevent an autopsy of Ishi's body, since that violated Ishi's spiritual beliefs, by sending a telegram to Gifford, regarding this possibility: "If there is any talk of the interests of science," he wrote, "say for me that science can go to hell." But it arrived too late; the autopsy was performed at the UC Hospital shortly after Ishi died. His brain was also removed, and his body embalmed. The doctors couldn't care less about Ishi's spiritual beliefs, and probably had no knowledge of them to boot.

The film invents a number of scenarios that never actually happened, but are creatively used to elaborate important issues. For example, in one scene, the two of them are sitting side by side. Kroeber is holding a notebook, as he is planning to write a bk about Ishi. He senses Ishi is angry at him. Ishi touches the notebook, and asks Kroeber: "Is Ishi here?" Kroeber says yes. Then Ishi touches the place over Kroeber's heart, and says, rather sadly, "Not here." It is unlikely that such an exchange ever took place, but it captures a great truth. It dramatizes a key difference between civilization and non-civilization. The West wants to be an objective observer, period; no heart stuff need apply. In this way, the movie is a profound indictment of

Western, and especially American, culture. (To his credit, Kroeber never wrote the planned book.)

Has any of this changed since Ishi died, or since Kroeber became a psychoanalyst? We can of course point to the rebellion of the sixties, the interest in Eastern philosophy and meditation, the popularity of New Age spirituality, and so on, but come on: just look around. One could easily argue that the brutality of contemporary America, and certainly its current administration, has never been uglier, or more intense. America is essentially about predation, exploitation, and unchecked narcissism. So please don't talk to me about Carlos Castaneda, or ayahuasca retreats in Arizona. The baldfaced truth is that we haven't learned a thing. The alternative possibility that Sackman wrote about (above) is a nonstarter for America and most Americans. We will pursue our callous way of life until it does us in. Arnold Toynbee put it quite unequivocally: civilizations tend to die by committing suicide.

## CHAPTER 4

# RUTH BENEDICT

Culture is personality writ large.

—Ruth Benedict, *Patterns of Culture* (1934)

It is curious to see how the basic patterns of our lives hold from babyhood to decrepitude.

—Ruth Benedict, journal fragment, ca. 1935

Ruth Benedict, as an anthropologist and keen observer of human behavior, became very famous in her lifetime, like her student, Margaret Mead. Scholars of academic disciplines don't typically become household words; they did. Their work, which (as already noted) sold in the millions, echoes down through the decades, and is still relevant today. Like Kroeber, they were mentored by Franz Boas (one begins to wonder whom he *didn't* teach), and he taught them well. His own work and conceptual outlook served as launching pads for their own careers, which ultimately outdid his in terms of visibility and probably, in influence as well. For the two of them offered powerful analyses of what human beings—and human societies—are all about, and the resulting debates on the subject were hardly confined to academic journals.(1)

Let's start with Ruth, then. She is best known for two books: *Patterns of Culture*, and *The Chrysanthemum and the Sword*—each of them a tour de force. The point of these books, and indeed of her entire intellectual career, was to argue, and demonstrate, that "normal" and "abnormal" were relative terms; that they were culturally defined, nothing more. Obviously, she was fully within the Boasian mold. Recall our discussion in Chapter 2 of how Mexicans eat insects while Americans find this distasteful, or how (Eastern) Indians mostly go in for arranged marriages while Westerners tend to be enraptured (captivated, transported, enthralled) by the ideal of romantic love.(2) It's all arbitrary, said Benedict; there simply is no "correct" value system, no "right" way to live. Before I elaborate further on her two major books, however, it will be worth our while to do a brief background profile on her.

Ruth was born in New York City in 1887, and graduated from Vassar College in 1909, where her classmates labeled her an "intellectual radical." In fact, she always saw herself as an outsider, a marginal person in American society; being bisexual had a lot to do with it. Years later, she began graduate work at Columbia University, and received her Ph.D. in anthropology in 1923, at which time she became a member of the faculty. Ruth was partially deaf, due to having contracted measles as an infant. She got married in 1914, and separated from her husband several years later. She had a very close friendship with

Margaret Mead, which was both intellectual and romantic in nature (more on this in Chapter 5). She also had a brief affair with Edward Sapir, and, as of 1931, a very happy relationship with a medical student named Natalie Raymond, which lasted until 1938. Her final romantic relationship was with a psychologist named Ruth Valentine. In 1931 Boas appointed her assistant professor; the two of them ran the department during 1932-35. Her first book, *Tales of the Cochiti Indians* (1931), and her subsequent *Zuñi Mythology* (1935), were based on eleven years of fieldwork among, and research into, the Zuñi, Apache, Blackfoot, and Shoshonean Serrano peoples. Ruth was editor of the *Journal of American Folklore* during 1925-40; in 1947 she was elected president of the American Anthropological Association. During her lifetime, she received numerous awards and accolades; in 1995, her image was put on a 46-cent stamp. Ruth died in 1948; she remains one of the great figures of American intellectual history and social science.

In what follows I am going to say a few words about her most famous work, *Patterns of Culture*, and then speculate on the impetus behind it—and indeed, behind her fierce commitment to cultural relativism in general. Just to jump ahead for a moment, Margaret Caffrey, in her biography of RB, says that one motivation for the book was a "simple theme" that lay at the heart of it, namely the struggle between the individual and their culture, in particular when you don't fit in, when you recognize that you are an outsider, even a misfit; when you are at odds with your culture's values. This was the crux of the matter. On some level, outsiders really do want to fit in, be accepted.

In any case, says Caffrey, *Patterns* "appeared on the scene as a burst of light." Reviewers fell over themselves praising it. In fact, the book got translated into fourteen languages, and became a standard university textbook. Boas wrote the Introduction; Mead wrote the Preface. Anthropology was off and running in a new direction; the field would never be the same again. What, exactly, was Ruth saying?

"A culture, like an individual," she wrote, "is a more or less consistent pattern of thought and action." From a large number of human possibilities, each culture chooses only a few characteristics, and these become its unique gestalt ("configuration"), as well as the traits of persons living in that culture. Each culture, in short, had a "modal personality," as it would later be called, a mode of being in the world that might have nothing in common with other cultures. She chose as examples the Kwakiutl of Vancouver Island, the Zuñi of New Mexico, and the Dobu of Papua New Guinea. So the dominant personality type among the Zuñi is characterized by moderation and harmony, while that of the Kwakiutl by competition and aggression—the modal personality being a megalomaniac, in other words —and that of the Dobu by paranoia and suspicion. Cultural relativism dictated that any given culture can only be understood from the inside, i.e., in its own terms, rather than through the "lens" of an outside culture. This led to a discussion of "abnormal" behavior. As she said in an essay she published two years earlier, "Anthropology and the Abnormal"—her agenda was really to render homosexuality normal—something like trance practice, let's say, was regarded as a sign of mental illness in the West, whereas in some native societies it was "the door to prestige as a shaman or tribal leader." This was "personality writ large." Normality, she concluded, in the essay and the book, was culturally defined. And if one didn't conform to the modal personality of their culture, they became a misfit, an outcast—like herself, although she didn't say so.

Much of the impetus behind *Patterns* was her opposition to homophobia, and the stigma attached to homosexual relations. This had a lot to do with her deep commitment to cultural relativism, and her argument that "normal" was culturally defined. She wanted Americans to see through their own culture, their own motivations; to become aware of their cultural conditioning, and free themselves from stereotypical thinking. As a professor, she pressed her students to try to understand versions of reality that were different from their own. As I said above, outsiders want more than anything to be accepted, and Ruth wanted that more than anything.

In any case, *Patterns* was not without its critics. Attacks on it went on even after her death. The book was too subjective, unscientific, intuitive, and so on. There is no need to review this material here, except to note an odd aspect of it: repeatedly, observes Margaret Caffrey, a number of anthropologists discredited her cultural description, and then ended their critiques "by accepting the premises on which that description was built." One anthropologist, Adamson Hoebel, wrote such an article in 1954, concluding his list of all of the book's supposed flaws by saying that in it, Ruth had contributed "theory and methodological devices of...great import and lasting value." In fact, in her presidential address to the American Anthropological Association in 1947, she told her audience that the field needed to accept not only quantitative evidence, but also qualitative evidence. Kroeber backed her up, essentially arguing for the existence of subjective facts. In his review of the book, he said that the approach was that of finding the "genius" of a culture, and that it was OK that this could not be measured. Science, he said, did not admit the validity of a "subjective empirical approach"; the research had to be done "primarily by feeling."

(It is interesting to note that decades later, Robert Pirsig, in *Zen and the Art of Motorcycle Maintenance*, argued for the existence of subjective truth—he called it "Quality," something that was felt—and went insane trying to get the culture to recognize it. Presumably he never read RB's work; he could have saved himself the trouble.)

Let us, then, have a look at Ruth's other great book, her cultural analysis of Japan: *The Chrysanthemum and the Sword*, which was published in 1946. During the War, the government commissioned her to investigate the national character of the Japanese, so that the US could better prosecute the War and the subsequent Occupation. Her anthropological assessment included the following points:

-The Japanese believe in the primacy of spirit over matter. They saw the war as a conflict between their own faith in the Japanese spirit vs. the American faith in matériel and technology. For the Japanese, the spirit is eternal; matter just comes and goes.

-The Japanese believe in the primacy of the group or community over the individual, and in hierarchy over equality. Whereas in the West, it is seen as a sign of strength to rebel against conventions, in Japan this is regarded as a sign of immaturity. For the Japanese, the strong are those who conform, fulfill their obligations, know their place in the hierarchy, and follow the accepted social code. Along with this, she noted that for Americans, competition was a way of life, whereas the Japanese strove to minimize it.

-Japan is a shame-culture, whereas America is a guilt-culture. In other words, the Japanese rely on external sanctions (such as fear of ridicule) for appropriate behavior; Americans, on the other hand, have an internalized notion of sin. Japanese ethics are thus what might be called "situational."

*The Chrysanthemum and the Sword* was a runaway best-seller in Japan, whereas American interest was largely confined to academic (and government) circles. By 1999 the book had sold more than 2.3 million copies in Japanese translation, and a survey conducted in 1987 revealed that more than one-third of the Japanese public had heard of it. It is even quoted in Japanese high school textbooks, and often assigned as a college text. There was a general consensus in Japan, despite a number of criticisms of the work, and the fact that Benedict did not read or speak Japanese, that "she got us right." The Japanese looked on Ruth's list of Japanese national characteristics with pride; the feeling was, Yes, this is the real Japan. To this day, the book is regarded as a classic.

In addition, the book served up an interesting twist on reality, one pointed out by the anthropologist Clifford Geertz. The structure of Ruth's analysis, he wrote, was that of "Us/Not-Us," with "Not-Us"—which is to say, Japanese culture—starting to look superior by the time you got to the end of the book! Her rhetorical strategy was to juxtapose the all-too-familiar with the supposedly exotic, such that they finally change places, and "Us" is the nation that gets called into question. By the end, says Geertz, the enemy who at the beginning of the book is the most alien we ever fought, proves to be the most reasonable we ever fought, and we Americans are left to reflect on our alleged cultural "certainties." This is, of course, vintage Benedict. The overall effect is to invert our perception: it is we who come off looking strange. If this is a profound insight, it is also an amusing one.

Which brings me to the issue of what America is all about. In the last analysis, what did Ruth really accomplish? It was her belief that once Americans examined themselves and their own culture, acquired some degree of introspection, of self-transparency, they would then be able and willing to move the culture in a positive direction; social engineer it, as it were. This never happened.(3) In fact, one might argue that the American pattern, or configuration—its "genius"—is precisely the ability to block out any such activity. The position of America—it's a kind of reflex reaction, really—has always been that we are the innocents, the aggrieved party, and that if anything bad happens, it's the other guy's fault. In the eighty or so years since the death of FDR, every president except for Jimmy Carter took that position; Trump is merely the latest expression of it. In Carter's 1979 Annapolis "spiritual malaise" speech, he said we can't keep blaming the Soviet Union for our problems, and he quoted the bible, the famous line about "the mote in one's eye." A note on the Internet parses this as follows:

"'The mote in one's eye' refers to a small fault or imperfection that a person notices in someone else, while ignoring a much larger fault in themselves. It's a metaphor, often found in religious texts, highlighting the tendency to judge others harshly for minor flaws while overlooking one's own significant shortcomings.

"The phrase is most famously used in the biblical passage Matthew 7:3-5, where Jesus criticizes those who focus on the 'mote' (a small speck of dust or sawdust) in their brother's eye while ignoring the 'beam' (a large piece of timber) in their own eye. This parable emphasizes the dangers of hypocrisy and self-righteousness, urging individuals to address their own flaws before attempting to correct others."

It is hardly surprising that the American people subsequently voted Carter out of office by the greatest electoral landslide in American history, preferring a willfully blind individual—a man who epitomized who they themselves were—who referred to Russia as the "evil empire," and to America as the (shining) "city on the hill." Clearly, the hopes of the cultural relativists were much too idealistic to be realized. The depressing truth about the United States is that willful blindness *is* the American pattern. In that regard, things have only gotten worse since Ruth died: Korea, Vietnam, Iraq, Afghanistan, the destruction of democracies (Guatemala, Iran), the support of dictatorships, and so on. "Don't stretch me out on the couch," declared Bush Sr.; I have absolutely no interest in introspection, in finding out who I am. My guess is that he spoke for the great majority of Americans.

Ruth Benedict was a fabulous human being, an inspiration to us all, endlessly trying to get us to look at ourselves from the outside, as it were, in the hope that social change might happen as a result. But here, I confess that I am a bit confused about what she ultimately believed in, and I'm not sure whether the confusion is within me or within Ruth. If we consider the two epigraphs at the head of this chapter, we are presented with a conundrum. Culture is personality writ large—is personality mapped onto culture, in other words—*and*, personalities don't really change that much from cradle to grave. Then how is her program of effecting deep positive changes in a culture supposed to take place? By her own admission, the basic patterns of our lives never change—something any competent psychotherapist will tell you is true. Talking to various therapists over the years, I discovered they all agree on this: we evolve, we (hopefully) smooth off the rough edges of our personality as the years go by, but the fundamental patterns that get laid down by age five, or seven—well, as Ruth says, they hold. Alteration of the basic framework in an individual personality pretty much takes an act of God; how much more so, alteration of the basic framework of an entire society? Clearly, social engineering has its limits. The poet Weldon Kees nailed it quite definitively in an essay he published in the *New Republic* (18 July 1955), in which he asserted that self-knowledge simply wouldn't do the trick; that it could not save us from a world filled with "violence and irrationality, with so many human beings murdering themselves, either literally or symbolically."

Wise words, looking back; prescient words, if we look ahead from that date seventy-plus years.

And yet, Ruth, along with Boas and Mead and all of the cultural relativists, were dedicated to the notion that self-transparency would lead to major social changes. Were they nuts? Is this an extreme case of cognitive dissonance? After all, in the hundred-plus years since Ruth got her Ph.D., things have gotten demonstrably worse, on a worldwide basis. (This is surely not something I have to document.) For large-scale societal change does not occur as the result of exhortation, or deeply felt intention, or incremental improvement, or individuals becoming self-transparent—mostly changes in consciousness, as it were. That's not how history works. (*How* it works would require a whole other discussion, but see the hint provided at the end of the Epilogue, below.) Ruth was hardly a fool, and if she were to return from the dead and have a look around, I'm pretty sure she would say something like this: "Gee, I guess I was wrong."

But I think she might add the following: "I tried as hard as I could, and I can't avoid feeling that the struggle was worth it." What more than that can any of us say, really?

## Chapter 5

# Margaret Mead

Perhaps the most influential public figure in the history of anthropology.

—Thomas Hylland Eriksen and Finn Sivert Nielsen, *A History of Anthropology*

We are faced with the problem of building a new world.

—Margaret Mead and Gregory Bateson, 1942

A joke began to circulate [in the late sixties]: What did Margaret Mead say when she was introduced to the Delphic Oracle? She said, "Hello, isn't there something *you'd* like to know?"

—Jane Howard, *Margaret Mead*

She was almost as much of a powerhouse as Franz Boas. She was a one-woman campaign to change the world. Her message was simple: if culture shapes personality, then personality can be changed by changing culture. *Coming of*

*Age in Samoa* (1928) was among the most widely read books ever written by an anthropologist. During her lifetime (1901-78) she wrote thirty-four books, made ten films, received twenty-eight honorary degrees, and collected a large number of awards and appointments, including the presidency of the American Association for the Advancement of Science in 1975. A student of Boas and Benedict, she received her Ph.D. in 1929. She was mentor to many young anthropologists and sociologists, and taught at the New School, Columbia, Fordham, and the University of Rhode Island. She was married to Gregory Bateson during 1936-50, and had a deep intellectual and romantic relationship with Ruth Benedict. In 1998, her face appeared on the 32-cent stamp.(1)

To say she conducted a "campaign" is no exaggeration; "crusade" would be more like it. Mead believed that patterns of racism, war, and environmental destruction were only habits, and that we were capable of building new ones. To that end, she was constantly in the public eye: TV interviews, public lectures, eighteen years of posting a monthly column in *Redbook* (read by millions), books, articles, and so on. Her favorite topics included women's rights, child-rearing, sexual morality, nuclear proliferation, race relations, drug addiction, population control, environmental pollution, and world hunger. She advised government agencies and testified before Congress. Betty Friedan's attack on her in *The Feminine Mystique* (1963) only served to increase her visibility. She appeared six times on "The Tonight Show," with Johnny Carson; *Time* magazine called her "Mother to the World." Following her death in 1978, eulogies poured in by the boatload. "If you took the best ten percent that Mead has done," wrote Alfred Kroeber, "you'll find it's more in quantity and better in quality than most other anthropologists."

*Coming of Age in Samoa* was an outstanding success, commercially and otherwise. Rave reviews came in from a star-studded cast: Havelock Ellis, Bronislaw Malinowski, and H.L. Mencken, among others. The book generated enormous excitement, nationwide, and over the years it sold millions of copies. So we need to ask: What was all the excitement about?

Mead did nine months of fieldwork among a small group of Samoans, a village of 600 people, with whom she lived in 1925. She endeared herself to the people, and recorded a large amount of ethnographic data. She wrote about how Samoan children were raised and educated, and how the women matured into old age. She also studied Samoan dances, personality development, modes of conflict resolution, and so on. But her major focus was child and adolescent sexuality. With the help of an interpreter, she interviewed sixty-eight girls/women between the ages of ten and twenty. Her conclusion: Adolescence for these girls and young women

> represented no period of crisis or stress, but was instead an orderly development of a set of slowly maturing interests and activities. The girls' minds were perplexed by no conflicts, troubled by no philosophical inquiries, beset by no remote ambitions.
>
> To live as a girl with many lovers as long as possible and then to marry in one's own village, near one's own rela-

tives and to have many children, these were uniform and satisfying ambitions.

Samoans, she added, had no notion of romantic love, such as it exists in the West.

What Mead was effectively telling her readers was that Samoa did sex "right," whereas America did it all wrong. Premarital sex in Samoa was fairly common; Samoan girls were allowed to explore their sexuality in secrecy through tacit sexual encounters. As for homosexuality, it was casually accepted, seen as a kind of play.

It was Mead's stark comparison that got Americans all worked up. The transition from childhood to adolescence in Samoa, she wrote, was a smooth one, not characterized by the distress/confusion/anxiety that was present in the United States. The American situation, she asserted, was constrained and awkward. The Samoan system of morality, so different from the puritanical American one, meant that the transition there would not be stressful. Adolescent Samoan girls did not experience lots of psychological tension; things were more or less relaxed. This meant, of course, that adolescent crises were not universal, but culturally conditioned, thereby lending further credence to the Boasian argument for cultural relativism. The final two chapters of the book were added at the suggestion of her publisher, William Morrow, which, writes her biographer Jane Howard, "raised issues that would still be debated long after her death." For example, she thought the American pattern of the nuclear family gave rise to "crippling attitudes" (Mead's words), whereas her own preference was for the extended family pattern of the

Samoans, which (she claimed) did not. Morrow's commercial instincts were right; "ideas like these," writes Howard,

> would help find a vast and receptive audience for her book, in which she had also portrayed a romantic paradise of a place where no one ever had acne or blushed from embarrassment or squirmed from frustration. If the Samoans could live so happily, she strongly hinted, perhaps North Americans could too.

All of this was in 1928. Counterclaims to this rosy picture by other anthropologists, namely that issues of sex and adolescence were basically the same in Samoa and America, were long in coming. Skipping ahead fifty-five years, Mead found herself posthumously attacked by a New Zealand anthropologist named Derek Freeman, in *Margaret Mead and Samoa: The Unmaking of an Anthropological Myth* (1983), which argued that Mead had got it all wrong; that Samoan youths suffered from the same problems that Western youths did. Freeman had a lot of expertise in the subject. In 1939, he won an appointment as a teacher in the Education Department of Samoa, and became fluent in the language. Like Mead, he also lived among them—in his case, much longer than she did—and was adopted by a Samoan family. He also did a teaching stint at the University of Samoa. So he couldn't be dismissed as a hack, although (see below) he appears to have been something of a nut job. In any case, his alleged discrediting of Mead made major headlines when the book was published, and led to a reconsideration of her work. Freeman went on a publicity tour of the US, which included interviews on CBS Morning News and the Phil

Donahue Show. This was followed by a second broadside in 1998, *The Fateful Hoaxing of Margaret Mead*. The debates were hot and heavy; as far as I know, the jury is still out on the question of the validity of Mead's claims vs. those of Freeman's. Let me briefly summarize the argument, and then comment on what the implications are for the nature vs. nurture debate and the issue of social change.

Just a coda, before I turn to Freeman's attack: the man comes off as a bit over the top; even, perhaps, deranged. Commentators on him, and his work, described it as "venomous" and "virulent," adding that he had a messianic complex. (He too was on a crusade.) He was known to have a rather violent personality, given to fierce antagonisms, and he suffered three major nervous breakdowns. In one case he broke into the museum in Sarawak and smashed a carved wooden sculpture, an erotic statue, which was a religious icon of the Iban people. Apparently, Freeman believed that the museum's curator, a man named Tom Harrisson, whom Freeman despised as a scholarly rival, was working with the Soviet Union to subvert the British rule in Malaysia, and was exerting a form of mind control over him. (One has to wonder: *The Manchurian Candidate* appeared in movie theaters at around this time.) This led him to consult a psychiatrist in Canberra, who evaluated him as being emotionally unstable. Freeman then wrote a report, denouncing the doctor as incompetent. In fact, his friends and colleagues had long wondered about his mental health. In another case, this time in Samoa, the natives found him wandering the beach in an agitated state. He became verbally violent; the coast guard picked him up, and took him to the local hospital. (The Samoans thought his erratic behavior was the result of spirit possession.) "The personality he projects," wrote Margaret's daughter in 1984, "is equally antithetical to hers—rigid and grim and competitive." "Full of accumulated venom," is how she described him at another point. She met Freeman on a televised debate; during a commercial break, he took the opportunity to sneer at her. To put it bluntly, Derek Freeman was an asshole.

Of course, none of this means that he couldn't be right in his critique of Mead, but it does cast doubt on his judgment. Here are the two major points of that critique:

-Mead was projecting her own romantic desires onto the adolescent Samoan girls; she wanted to see them as sexually liberated, for her own psychological reasons. The truth was that Samoan sex life was not as free and easy as she depicted it. In general, he claimed, Samoans were rigid and competitive; jealousy, and even rape, were common, along with juvenile delinquency and suicide.

-She was hoaxed by two of her informants, who were playing a joke on her, telling her how they had lots of sex with boys as teenagers when they actually hadn't. This deception, according to Freeman, was what launched Mead's book.

What to make of this? In the years following the publication of Freeman's books, scholarly opinion was heavily divided on the issue of who was right. The American Anthropological Association declared that the first book was "poorly written, unscientific, irresponsible, and misleading." The president of the Association, Louise

Lamphere, reacted to Freeman's death in 2001 with a letter to the *New York Times*:

> I have taught about the controversy for the last 18 years and am still impressed by the fact that a 24-year-old woman could produce a study so far ahead of its time. Dr. Freeman studied a different island 20 years after Mead's research, and his notion that biology is more determinative than culture is oversimplified. Most serious scholarship casts grave doubt on his data and theory.

Nevertheless, a survey of 301 anthropologists in the US, taken in 2016, had two thirds declaring that Mead "romanticizes the sexual freedom of Samoan adolescents" (which could be true) and half asserting that her work was ideologically motivated (which was certainly true). In anthropological circles, at least, arguments and data went back and forth; doubt was cast on the empirical basis of both their works.

Meanwhile, it turns out that Freeman's "joke" theory doesn't hold water; it was completely discredited by Martin Orans, a distinguished professor of anthropology, in 1996, and by an expert on Samoan culture, Paul Shankman, in his study of 2009: *The Trashing of Margaret Mead*. Shankman concluded that Margaret's research was essentially correct, and that Freeman cherry-picked his data so as to misrepresent, and discredit, her work. On this point, at least, Freeman was clearly over the top.

In the Epilogue to her memoir about her parents, *With a Daughter's Eye*, Mary Catherine Bateson defended her mother's work against Freeman, pointing out, for example, that his characterization of cultural anthropologists was a distortion. Specifically, she said, they did not dismiss biology as a factor in human behavior. To some extent, he was setting up a straw man.

That being said, it seems to me that ideology and emotion did play decisive roles in the fieldwork and research of both of our protagonists. As editor Sam Dresser tells it, both Freeman and Mead went to Samoa wearing tinted lenses. Mead wanted to provide support for Boas' theories and the "school" of cultural relativism; Freeman wanted to discredit Mead, and argue that biology, not culture, ruled the day. To switch metaphors, they both had axes to grind; both had been described by friends and colleagues as "messianic." Mead dedicated her life to the (Boasian, Benedictian) proposition that society was malleable, could be changed for the better. Freeman was a conservative: if biology is the determining factor for human beings, then fundamental change is not terribly likely.

What should we say about biology vs. cultural conditioning? As Ruth Benedict admitted, people don't really change very much. Consider the epigraph to this chapter: Margaret did not manage to build a new world. She didn't even come close. As a young woman, according to Benjamin Breen (in *Tripping on Utopia*), she recognized that her worst trait was "a dangerous tendency to make sweeping claims about world-changing breakthroughs based on scanty evidence" (Breen's paraphrase). A decent argument can be made for human inflexibility, it seems to me.

However, Mead wasn't necessarily wrong; or maybe we should say, she was incomplete, and who of us isn't? Because the current status of the nature/nurture debate has it that both factors are at play; that genes and the environment work together in a complex interaction. A compromise, then; it's not an either/or situation. As for the issue of social change based on self-knowledge: what I said above, at the conclusion of Chapter 4, I think applies to the aspiration of Margaret Mead as well: it's a long shot.

Setting that aside, let me close this chapter with the words on Margaret's tombstone: "To cherish the life of the world." And she did do that, didn't she?

## Chapter 6

# Gregory Bateson

Let me state my belief that such matters as the bilateral symmetry of an animal, the patterned arrangement of leaves in a plant, the escalation of an armaments race, the processes of courtship, the nature of play, the grammar of a sentence, the mystery of biological evolution, and the contemporary crises in man's relationship to his environment, can only be understood in terms of such an ecology of ideas as I propose.

—Gregory Bateson, *Steps to an Ecology of Mind*

We are most of us governed by epistemologies that we know to be wrong.

—Gregory Bateson, *Steps to an Ecology of Mind*

To have a vision of the world one's fellow men do not share is lonely and even frightening. . . Gregory Bateson has been blessed, and cursed, with a mind that sees through things to a world of pattern and form that lies beyond.

—Roger Keesing, 1974 review of *Steps to an Ecology of Mind*

Before attempting an explication of Gregory Bateson's work, I need to inject three notes here, or *avisos*, as we say in Spanish. As follows:

1. This is on the order of a personal note. I lived in San Francisco between 1975 and 1980. I studied Bateson's work during that time, and also wrote it up during that time, in a book that was published in 1981, *The Reenchantment of the World*. In the spring of 1980, a mutual friend of ours was in the process of setting up a meeting between myself and Gregory. Then, in July of 1980, he died, and I missed my chance. I have always felt bad about this, first because he was only seventy-six, and should have lived longer, and second because he was a great thinker, and I'm sure I could have learned much from him. *C'est la vie*.

2. Another personal note: In the fall of 1975, I was in London for a few weeks, finishing the details on what would be a previous book (*Social Change and Scientific Organization*, 1978), and happened to see a notice that GB would be giving a public lecture—I forget now where it was being held—which would be chaired by R.D. Laing. I got there a bit early, and sat towards the front. It was a very large auditorium, and eventually the audience probably amounted to more than a thousand people. Laing introduced the speaker, who then began a rambling discourse that was hard to follow. He seemed to be going nowhere. After five minutes of this, a man in his late twenties stood up, and said, quite loudly, something like "Could you get to the point?" Laing immediately got up, came to the lectern,

46

and said to the young man, "I'm sorry, but we're here to hear Gregory Bateson." The man then replied, again very loudly, "Why does he have to be so boring?" After that he sat down, as did Laing, and Gregory went on with his talk.

Of course, the man who interrupted Gregory was extremely rude—what could have been his motivation?—but, I reflected later on, he was right: it was not at all clear what Bateson was trying to say, and as a result he did come across as rather dull. Or at the very least, enigmatic, possibly even incoherent. This was unfortunately something of a Batesonian "trademark." From which it follows:

3.Gregory was not a linear thinker. He tended to think in terms of analogies, following the pattern laid out in what he called the "schizophrenic syllogism" (men are grass; see below). For our purposes, I tried to render his ideas in a linear fashion, and was pretty much thwarted in this effort. As a result, my own thinking, at least in this chapter, would also seem to follow the schizophrenic mode; it tends to wander a bit. That being said, let me list what I see as the major themes in or about GB's work:(1)

-The influence of his father, William Bateson

-The need for a new epistemology, because that of the West was in "runaway"

-Everything is structurally related to everything else

-His mode of thinking was brilliantly intuitive

-But it was very weak, empirically speaking

-His mode of communication was esoteric, enigmatic, and in general very hard to follow

In a certain sense, Bateson is the odd man out in this collection of profiles, because he was not opposed to civilization per se, and he never believed in "primitive" solutions for the West. His target was a lot broader: a critique of our entire way of thinking, which is to say, of Western epistemology *in toto*. How to describe this intellectual activity? Adjectives that have been applied to him, his work, and his mode of thinking, include eclectic, elusive, puzzling, systemic, holistic, ecological, intoxicating, and interdisciplinary. Innovative concepts flew off him like sparks off a birthday cake (of an octogenarian), and as a result he influenced a great number of students and researchers in a variety of disciplines.

It's no accident that he died in a Zen center (San Francisco), for his work does have a kind of buddhistic flavor to it. He saw reality as essentially relational; he believed everything was interconnected. His explicit goal was not to change the world, but to change us *in* the world, which might then change the world, as his wife, Margaret Mead, and other cultural relativists were trying to do. He pretty much left the (social, physical) world as he found it, but he did endow us with an alternative way of relating to it, one that might conceivably be better than the one we've got now. But it never got implemented, except in some professional circles, such as psychology (e.g., family therapy) and cybernetics (of which he was later critical). Consider the epigraph to this chapter: Do most of us in the Western world really know, or believe, that our epistemologies are wrong? I tend to doubt it.

In addition, there is a tendency for holistic systems to become closed, turn in on themselves, rendering them impervious to criticism, or Popperian-style falsification; which raises the question as to whether we would in fact be better off living in a Batesonian world, to coin a phrase. A clear indication of this hermetic characteristic, which I have observed over the years, is the employment of a private language, spoken by an in-crowd, which turned Bateson's ideas into slogans and buzzwords. This is reflected in his entry on Wikipedia, which states that in academic circles he was a kind of "cult figure whose appeal includes his obscurity [and] eccentricity." These folks had, in effect, created a religion, an alternative universe, in much the same way that Eric Hoffer characterized "true believers." Systems theory was The Answer. Most of them had left critical thinking far behind; they could think holistically, in the cult jargon of systems theory, but not in any other way. In the seventies, that bible of the counterculture, *The Whole Earth Catalog*, was shot through with adulation for Bateson, and he had by this time become something of a "reluctant therapist to an entire generation," as Benjamin Breen put it. Writing in 2006, and looking back on the Bateson-worship of the seventies, Australian psychiatrist Brian Stagoll talks about "the twin mistakes of deifying him as a transcendent figure…or reifying his ideas into mechanistic slogans."(2) I'm not sure what Bateson thought of his guru-like status in his later years, but just as Marx was finally forced to declare, *Je ne suis pas une marxiste*, Gregory might have privately said to himself, "I'm not a Batesonian." (Word has it that he didn't think much of the counterculture.) All of this makes it hard to evaluate his legacy. It is, beyond a doubt, quite impressive, but he did have a tendency to talk in a way that was cryptic; like the Delphic Oracle, one might say.

That students and colleagues couldn't understand him is a recurrent theme in studies of his work and in audiences who heard him lecture, and it is connected to the problem of an absence of empirical data on his part. I hasten to add that this cryptic quality is very different from the jargon of postmodern deconstructionism, which strikes me as being cryptic for its own sake, and ultimately empty. As an old joke has it: What do you get when you cross a postmodern deconstructionist with a mafioso? Answer: Someone who makes you an offer you can't understand. Even if often incomprehensible, GB doesn't fall into this category.

In any case, friends and colleagues observed the following:

-When Gregory was scheduled to lecture, he often dropped the advertised topic and engaged in improv instead.

-In 1949, his major institutional connection was to the V.A. Hospital in Menlo Park. Most of the psychiatric residents were not able to understand him, and often asked him, directly, "What are you talking about?"

-When he was working on the double bind theory (see below), his colleagues didn't know what to make of his ideas. One of them, Jay Haley, wrote: "we were trying to figure out what on earth Gregory was talking about...He never had any data." Haley went on to say that the theory was something he just pulled out of the sky. In fact, Gregory's "evidence" consisted of anecdotes.

-Two psychiatrists in St. Louis wrote that the double bind theory failed to agree with their clinical data. In fact, they reported that the theory made it worse for the parents of schizophrenics.

-In 1969, the National Institute of Mental Health (NIMH) withdrew its funding for him, saying that his science was not based on experimental or clinical data.

Comments like this were pretty typical. Let me provide another example, which is fairly iconic. This concerns the very last lecture Gregory ever gave, one month before he died. He was scheduled to deliver it at the annual meeting of a group called the Lindisfarne Association, based in Southampton, New York, in June of 1980, but by that time he was sinking fast, too ill to travel, so he taped the talk and sent it to Lindisfarne, for them to use as the keynote address. The title of the talk was "Men Are Grass: Metaphors and the World of Mental Process." This lecture is important for our purposes because Bateson explicitly states that it is "a survey of almost everything I've done in my life." What we are getting, then, is the essential Bateson, GB in a nutshell. The text of the lecture is nine pages long; the first six pages, not surprisingly enough, are rambling and incoherent—all over the place, as it were. But then, on the seventh page, he gets down to it. There is a syllogism, he says, that goes like this (originally set forth by Aristotle in the *Prior Analytics*, 350 B.C.):

Men die.
Socrates is a man.
[Therefore] Socrates will die.

Straightforward enough, it would seem; sound logical

reasoning. But then there is another syllogism, says Gregory, that goes like this (definitely not Greek in origin):

Grass dies.
Men die.
Men are grass.

Rather intriguing, no? Bateson says that recently, a British reviewer of his work "pointed out to me that most of my thinking takes the form of the second kind of sequence, and that would be all very well if I were a poet, but it is inelegant in a biologist." Now it's true, Gregory goes on, that the second syllogism certainly doesn't seem to be logical. In fact, a German-born American psychiatrist named Eilhard von Domarus wrote an essay called "Language and Thought in Schizophrenia," in which he noted that schizophrenics tend to talk and think "in syllogisms having the general structure of the syllogism in grass" (I'm quoting Bateson here).(3) The Socratic syllogism, says GB, is concerned with classes of things, whereas the grass syllogism is focused on the identification of predicates: dies—dies. That which dies is equivalent to the other thing that dies. Domarus claimed this was the way crazy people think—and also, poets; which, Bateson informs us, is the way *I* think. I think in terms of metaphor, he says, which is an *alternative* form of logic, "the logic upon which the biological world had been built." He refers here to homology, the similarity of body parts or structures across different species; the equivalency of predicates.(4)

Whew! Gregory was nothing if not mind-bending. I'm poorly versed in biology, but although it is important, I don't believe homology is the core of the biological world; in which case the leap from metaphor to biology would seem to be a bit of a stretch. Which would suggest that GB's British critic was right, the more so since the entities of the biological world—octopi, for example—are *material* entities, not poetic ones; unless they show up in the poems of Ogden Nash, or Shelley ("To a Skylark"—"Bird thou never wert"), or Edgar Allan Poe ("Nevermore!"). Or unless they can be described as "systems" (see below).

We see the issue at hand, then. If Bateson's analyses of various phenomena were conducted through the medium of a radically different epistemology, one of the "men are grass" variety, we would have entered a radically different world. Is it better than the one we've got? Or should poets stick to poetry, and biologists to biology? Different people will answer this question differently. It may depend on how poetic (or enigmatic) one wants to be. But let's dig a bit deeper into Batesonian thought. There might, after all, be a method to his madness.(5)

As it turns out, the apple didn't fall far from the proverbial tree. Gregory's father, the biologist William Bateson (he coined the term "genetics"), believed that emotion could be verified as precisely as reason. In 1891 he wrote: "If there had been no poets there would have been no problems, for surely the unlettered scientist of to-day would never have found them. To him it is easier to solve a difficulty than to feel it." Nearly fifty years later, the son would elaborate on this notion as follows:

> I picked up a vague mystical feeling that we must look for the same sort of processes in all fields of natural

phenomena—that we might expect to find the same sort of laws at work in the structure of a crystal as in the structure of society, or that the segmentation of an earthworm might really be comparable to the process by which basalt pillars are formed.

Also in 1891, William Bateson came up with a "Vibratory Theory of Repetition of Parts," which he described in a letter to his sister Anna as "the best idea I ever had." In this essay, he discussed "all the *patterns* and *recurrence of patterns* in animals and plants," referring to symmetry and "bilaterally symmetrical variation." In 1906 he wrote: "We commonly think of animals and plants as matter, but they are really systems through which matter is continually passing. The orderly relations of their parts are as much under geometrical control as the concentric waves spreading from a splash in a pool."

I think it fair to say that Gregory seems to have taken up from where his father left off.

Let me return to the issue of homologies. What would the practice of science consist of, based on these homologies, or "predicates"? Let's say you find similar laws at work in a piece of quartz and the structure of Bulgarian society, for example. Then what? This may be descriptive, but it doesn't seem to be predictive. Am I reading this right? It would seem to close a door, rather than open one. The historian of biology, William Coleman, wrote that for the father, there was a level of reality that went beyond the reach of scientific explanation; what the son would call Mind. This was an argument for necessary epistemological incompleteness, that the Mind could never know itself.(6)

There is a similarity here, it seems to me, to the work of Kurt Gödel (although Gregory never mentions him). At first glance, it looks as though Gödel's incompleteness theorems invalidated mathematics, shut it down. What they actually did was revolutionize the field, take it in new directions. Did the Batesons, father and son, have a similar impact on scientific inquiry? Did Gregory create a new science? That was certainly his goal. Barry Commoner, the biologist and environmentalist, said that the brilliance of Gregory was "that he senses the need of a new kind of 'thinking beast' in order to cope with the crisis that the world is in." Did he succeed? That, as Prince Hamlet said, is the question.

In this effort, his interest in cybernetics proved to be a great help. Mary Catherine Bateson, in her memoir of her parents, wrote that he was seeking to challenge the whole set of assumptions on which Western epistemology was built, and to find a new set, which would contain a self-correcting system—unlike that of Western epistemology, which he saw was caught up in "runaway," which is to say, self-destruction. Gregory believed that there were systems that contained built-in feedback loops that gave those systems the capacity for self-correction; which were, in other words, homeostatic.

Turning to his fieldwork: one of his more famous investigations dealt with a ceremony known as "naven," performed by the Iatmul people of New Guinea. His fieldwork there was conducted during the late twenties and early thirties, and resulted in his book, *Naven*, in 1936. During a second period he was accompanied by Margaret Mead, who introduced him to Ruth Benedict's concept of "pattern," which became central to his thinking. Ruth effectively served as a model for him, especially with her insistence that the anthropologist had to place him- or herself within the culture, not just observe it objectively. The naven ritual, which involves the switching of sex roles, looks pretty strange from the outside, whereas it makes perfect sense to the natives. An outside, sociological explanation, Bateson realized, didn't get you very far, because it omitted the most important thing, namely the emotional motivation of the participants. The key to the motives, he wrote, lay in the "ethos" of the culture, its emotional climate, so to speak; its pattern. Following Ruth's general argument about culture and personality, he said that culture "standardizes" the individual, molds his or her psychology.

All of this led to the formulation of one of Gregory's most famous anthropological concepts, that of schismogenesis. He coined the word to describe a vicious circle, a process of degenerative change. This phenomenon has a symmetrical form and a complementary form, and both build to a climax, or breaking point. A debate between two adversaries, for example, can escalate, get increasingly heated, until it results in a brawl. It turns out that the naven ceremony serves to defuse conflict within the culture, cool it off, as it were. In the absence of such stabilizing elements in any social situation, the system goes into "runaway." We see this, said GB, in the US-Russian arms race, which could potentially lead to war; or at an auction, when the urge to outbid the other person can render one of them broke.

In the case of the complementary variety, the rivalry is reciprocal; and Bateson gives as an example a common (at that time, but later as well) marital arrangement: dominant husband/submissive wife. Over time, the wife's submission provokes the husband's assertion, which encourages her submission, etc. Ultimately, neither of them can see the other's viewpoint. They both lose interest in making the relationship work. Reciprocal tensions continue to accumulate, until—very typically—the wife leaves the marriage. This single example, says Gregory, demonstrates a pattern that can be seen in a variety of situations, including politics, class conflict, and racial oppression. Theoretically, at least, this analysis renders us capable of dealing constructively with these situations. (A pity, Ruth might say, that people don't change.)

In the case of both types of schismogenesis, the ethos of either party doesn't exist independently, but is "cogged into" the ethos of the adversary. (Ethos = the set of attitudes and values of a community; its "character") As a result, all life situations have a grammar, or code. Individuals and societies, says GB, are organized entities; they are "coded" in a certain way that is coherent, that makes sense in both emotional and cognitive terms. How should we understand insanity, for example? It doesn't fall into a person's head, from out of the blue. You can only understand it, he asserts, if you take all of the participants, and their code of interaction, into account. Only then, as with schismogenic situations, are you in a position to do something about it.

This is a second famous concept of Bateson's, the "double bind" theory of schizophrenia. The question to ask in such a situation is, What is regular in the childhood of a schizophrenic? The pattern that got established, over many years, is that you must not comment on the messages of others made in the family situation. This results in weird forms of behavior and communication, which are employed in order to survive. They became the person's ethos, his or her character. It's a reaction to cultural norms, a patterned logical response that meshes with the family structure. In this situation, the metaphorical and the literal become confused, and the patient opts for metaphor because it's safer. Claiming he is Napoleon, for example.

The double bind consists precisely in this: the individual can't resolve his or her situation—is between a rock and a hard place—but in addition, they can't leave the field, because they need the vital connection to their parent. Declaring they are Napoleon is thus a way to leave the field, says GB. Madness, rather than being a breakdown of the psyche, is in fact a way of *salvaging* the psyche. In a word, says Bateson, there is no such thing as a schizophrenic person; there is only a schizophrenic *system*, or systemic network.

R.D. Laing summed up the double bind conundrum as follows: "Rule A: Don't. Rule A.1: Rule A does not exist. Rule A.2: Do not discuss the existence or nonexistence of Rules A, A.1, or A.2."

As it turns out, the double bind theory has been discredited as the sole explanation for schizophrenia. In particular, it lacked strong empirical support showing the links between double binds and madness. Nevertheless, according to a comment on the Internet,

Bateson's work on the double bind and the ecology of mind laid the groundwork for systemic family therapy, which views the family as a complex system where patterns of interaction influence individual behavior. This approach shifted the focus from treating individuals in isolation to addressing dysfunctional patterns of interaction within the family unit.

Once again, we see a persistent problem with Batesonianism: intuitively strong, empirically weak— perhaps, one might say, in the tradition of Mead, Benedict, and cultural relativism in general. The triumph here, if one can employ that term, is that in many quarters, madness is now treated via family therapy, not as an individual disease.

A third example of Batesonian thinking: optima vs. maxima. All living systems, says Bateson, are homeostatic; they seek to preserve themselves at an optimal point. Should they try to maximize any single variable, they will go into runaway, and destroy themselves and their immediate environment. Consider something as innocuous as vitamin or mineral supplements. We understand, for example, that the human body needs only so much calcium; that there is an optimal daily dosage for it. We do not say, "The more calcium I have in my body, the better off I'll be," because we understand that beyond a certain point, any chemical element becomes toxic. So we take one gram of calcium a day, let's say, not forty.

Our present dilemma, however, at least since the Industrial Revolution, comes out of the goal of unlimited expansion, maximizing profit in a capitalist economy. Here, we *do* say, "The more the better." The result? Capitalism has, for a long time now, been in runaway, and it is clearly destroying our lives, our environment, and—itself. On this point, Bateson and Marshall Sahlins (see below, Chapter 9) tend to converge. Efforts to halt this trajectory, such as the degrowth movement, have had limited success up to now.(7)

Or consider the field of politics. The will to power, Nietzsche called it. Demagogues and dictators wind up wrecking the body politic because of this lust, as can be seen in history and in contemporary America. And even in the realm of mental activity, since the Scientific Revolution, the West has tried to maximize reason above any other mode of thinking, and we are suffering from this lopsidedness as a result. "Everything in moderation," said Aristotle. Wise words, which we tend to ignore. (Runaway may be self-destructive, but it is definitely an adrenaline rush.)

I need to stop at this point. Bateson did so much, and in so many disciplines, that it would probably take an additional 200 pages (at least) to elaborate on his *oeuvre*. Topics of interest listed in one of his memos came to over 100 items. GB was a pioneer in LSD research, even setting up Allen Ginsberg with his first acid trip. He was a pioneer in the field of cybernetics. In ecology and environmental studies. In philosophy. In systems theory and communication theory. In ethology and ethnology. In organizational management. In anthropology. And all the while, managing to integrate these fields in an interdisciplinary way. "Bateson swam in all these vast currents," writes Brian Stagoll, "moving towards new aesthetic, holistic, and contextual forms of systemic wisdom." Technically an atheist, Gregory really did believe in "the sacred," which he defined as "a sense of the whole which can only be met with awe." It was, for him, immanent rather than transcendent. His youthful hero, his inspiration, was William Blake, and it seems fair to say that a Blakean outlook remained with him to the very end. We can be sure that he was familiar with Blake's famous painting of 1795, "Newton," which was the artist's critique of Enlightenment rationalism, and with Blake's poem of a few years later that ends, "May God us keep/From Single vision & Newtons sleep." (8)

To sum up: Gregory Bateson had one of the most fertile, and far-ranging, brains in the history of the human race, one hardly circumscribed by "Single vision." His legacy was enormous, but also, perhaps unavoidably, somewhat ambiguous. Let's face it: Western capitalism has hardly taken his advice regarding the importance of optima. Instead, it insists on pursuing the path of maxima, of runaway, to the very edge of the abyss and into it, which I believe is our future, at least in the short term. We are also not very Blakean, not into metaphor and mysticism, even though our commitment to scientism, if I may use that word, is finally taking us down a blind alley. Which leads me to the following speculative conclusion:

It is the argument of a number of scholars—Immanuel Wallerstein being notable among them—that we are, in the present century, moving out of the economic and geopolitical arrangements that have dominated the West since about 1500 A.D.(9) I have referred to this elsewhere as a "tectonic shift," which is defined in an Internet commentary as follows:

> A tectonic shift is the movement of Earth's tectonic plates, which are large segments of the planet's crust that float on the mantle. The term is also used metaphorically to describe fundamental and far-reaching changes in something, such as a business, technology, or society.

In other words, it is possible to "export" the phrase from geology to the social sciences, or politics, along the lines of a metaphor, or analogy. The current tectonic shift, it seems to me, is as massive as the previous one, namely the shift from the medieval to the modern world. I discuss this latter shift in *The Reenchantment of the World*, referred to above, in which I point out that there was a corresponding shift in the feudal epistemology—what might be called the magical world view—to the epistemology enshrined in the Scientific Revolution of the seventeenth century. It seems reasonable to expect that congruent with the current shift would be another epistemological shift, to something post-Western science. Bateson was pointedly seeking such an epistemology; it's really what his entire intellectual enterprise finally amounted to. That he didn't manage to go all the way, so to speak, shouldn't surprise us; such changes don't occur overnight, fully formed. He was *groping* toward it, which is probably, during his lifetime, the most we can expect. As an old Yiddish proverb has it, "To a fool you don't show a job half-done." In short, we probably need to cut Gregory some slack. Personally, I can't imagine a massive political and socioeconomic tectonic shift taking place without it being accompanied by a significant epistemological one. If we are going to live differently, doesn't it seem likely that we are going to think differently as well? What if men really did turn out to be grass, after all?(10)

## CHAPTER 7
# ZORA NEALE HURSTON

Prayer seems to me a cry of weakness, and an attempt to avoid, by trickery, the rules of the game as laid down. I do not choose to admit weakness. I accept the challenge of responsibility. Life, as it is, does not frighten me, since I have made my peace with the universe as I find it, and bow to its laws.

—Zora Neal Hurston, *Dust Tracks on a Road*

I belong to no race nor time. I am the eternal feminine with its string of beads...Sometimes, I feel discriminated against, but it does not make me angry. It merely astonishes me. How can any deny themselves the pleasure of my company?

—Zora Neale Hurston, "How It Feels to be Colored Me"

The story of Zora Neale Hurston (1891-1960) is a strange and outright unbelievable one, except for the fact that it's true. As a child she was raised in a small, all-black town in rural Florida, in complete obscurity. During her lifetime, she became a star of the Harlem Renaissance, and a close friend of Langston Hughes'; was a student of Franz Boas' at Barnard and Columbia, and worked with Ruth Benedict and Margaret Mead; was the recipient of a Guggenheim Fellowship, enabling her to do fieldwork in the American South, along with Jamaica and Haiti (where she met with zombies); was a great storyteller, raconteur, and truth-teller, beloved by practically everyone she met; got married and divorced three times; wrote seven books, the most famous of which, a novel called *Their Eyes Were Watching God*, sold more than a million copies; underwent a grueling initiation into the hoodoo cult of New Orleans; became a leading expert in Southern black folklore; and finally died in obscurity, was buried in an unmarked grave, and fell into oblivion, only to be rediscovered in 1975 by Alice Walker and subsequently get celebrated as one of the foremost female writers of the twentieth century. How she managed to do all that in a single lifetime, and post-lifetime, is beyond imagination. Obviously, this is one cameo that could easily turn into a full-blown biography. In what follows, I shall necessarily have to be rather selective about her life and work.(1)

Zora Neale had an enormous depth of feeling, about herself and the world around her. Hers was not a cerebral anthropology. Rather, it came from her heart, and her gut. But she was fundamentally a loner; as a child, she had prophetic visions that later came to pass. In her autobiography, *Dust Tracks on a Road*, she wrote, "A cosmic loneliness was my shadow." If her life played out on a large canvas, it was also shot through with a certain melancholy, one that makes her a very sympathetic figure.

Let's start with the hoodoo initiation in New Orleans. You want "participant observation"? Well, fasten your seat belts; here goes. But first, exactly what *is* hoodoo? This off the Internet:

> "Hoodoo" refers to a spiritual and magical practice of African American origin that combines elements of African religions, Native American beliefs, and European practices. It is mainly practiced in the southern United States and is characterized by its focus on the use of nature, spirits, and rituals to achieve various ends, such as protection, healing, justice, or love.

It was brought over to America by African slaves (also from Haiti and Martinique), who were knowledgeable in the ways of traditional native spiritual practices, to which they added Native American botanical knowledge. Tools of the trade, so to speak, include herbs, roots, oils, powders, and candles, used to cast spells. Practitioners are called root workers or conjure doctors. The practices were often held in secret, in black churches, which came to be called "the invisible institution." In the antebellum South, hoodoo was a form of resistance against slavery, and later, against white supremacy in general. In his autobiography, Frederick Douglass recounts how he sought spiritual assistance from an enslaved conjurer, who gave him a root to carry in his pocket for protection. Douglass subsequently defeated his slave master in a fight, and believed his victory was due to the talisman. In effect, at a basic level, hoodoo is a form of sympathetic magic (which could, of course, include a placebo effect).

According to Zora, by the early twentieth century New Orleans had become "the hoodoo capital of America," which included performing African dances in Congo Square, in the center of the old city. This is where she settled in to do her research. In fact, as someone who had had prescient visions as a girl, she was a believer in magic, and her fieldwork in New Orleans convinced her that the conjure tradition was "burning with a flame in America, with all the intensity of a suppressed religion." She found that (mostly black) people consulted hoodoo doctors for upset stomach, blindness, rheumatism, excessive menstrual bleeding, syphilis, broken hearts, legal matters, and general good luck. Also for finding a job, keeping a husband from straying, or to exact retribution for racial injustice that would never get a hearing in a Southern court. You name it, in other words. Her biographer, Valerie Boyd, writes that "hoodoo was an alternative form of power for people who might otherwise feel powerless. And when employed conscientiously, it was a restorative power, not a destructive one." "Hurston's research," she goes on to say, "corroborated what she already knew: Hoodoo was not mere superstition, and its potency was not imagined; it was real."

How, then, to study it? By total immersion, of course, which proved to be not for the faint of heart. Zora apprenticed herself to a number of hoodoo masters. Initiations typically involved celibacy, fasting, and ritual baths. In one case, she was required to lie on her couch for nine days and read the third chapter of Job, morning and night. It got much worse. In the case of the notorious "Black Cat Bone" ritual, she had to catch a black cat and throw it into a cauldron of boiling water. A bone of the cooked cat would then be carried around as a talisman, according to her teacher, Father Joe Watson, who was known throughout N'awlins as "the Frizzly Rooster." No chicken, however; he had great charisma, and empowered her "to work with the spirits anywhere on earth." Zora began to hold consultations on her own, such as helping a woman eject a bossy mother-in-law from her home (a frequent request, I'm guessing). In fact, she went for initiation to every conjurer she heard of, calling her approach "the vacuum method, grabbing everything I see."

This led her to the home of Luke Turner, who refused to accept any payment for his services. The initiation consisted of lying naked on Turner's couch, facedown, on top of a snake skin, for three days and three nights. During that time, she was to lie there, fasting, with only a bit of water at her side. She had a number of strange dreams. After sixty-nine hours and five psychic experiences, she awoke, with a feeling of exaltation. Turner then painted a large lightning symbol on her back, a pair of eyes on her cheeks, and the image of the sun on her forehead. He crowned her "the Rain-Bringer." By the end of 1928, writes Valerie Boyd, Zora knew more about hoodoo than any other scholar in the US. (She did write Boas about all this, but omitted the more harrowing details.) This became abundantly clear when, in 1931, she published a one-hundred-page article, "Hoodoo in America," in *The Journal of American Folk-Lore*, which was edited by her former professor at Barnard, Ruth Benedict.

And this was not the end of it. Four years later, Zora published *Mules and Men*, an anthropological triumph. Enhanced by a preface by Boas, it led to rave reviews, including one by Carl Sandburg. The book recounts her fieldwork in the South during the late twenties, and is part folklore and part hoodoo chronicle. She describes her initiations with the hoodoo masters of New Orleans, drawing on material from the 1931 essay. In addition, the book contains seventy Negro folktales. "It's fair to say," writes Valerie Boyd, "that no book...had ever given such precedence, such loving regard, to black speech; to what black people had to say, and *how* they said it...Hurston's skill at recording black dialect in *Mules and Men* is extraordinary." The book also disrupted the white stereotype of black people as mules, i.e., as little more than beasts of burden. "To the contrary," says Boyd, "her book showed them to be imaginative storytellers, clever songwriters, gifted healers, and inventive thinkers." One anthropologist, Melville Herskovits, wrote: "I think it is not saying too much to state that Miss Hurston probably has a more intimate knowledge of Negro folk life than anyone in this country."

The fallout was that Zora was awarded a Guggenheim Fellowship the following year, for "a study of magic practices among Negroes in the West Indies." Her wallet nicely filled out, she headed off to the Caribbean in April of 1936. In Jamaica, she met a group of Maroons, descendants of enslaved Africans who escaped from plantations and established autonomous communities. She began studying with their chief conjure doctor. One night, he ordered the thousands of croaking frogs in the bush to hush—which they did immediately. Then in September, she moved on to Haiti, and within a few months mastered Haitian Creole, acquired a working knowledge of the major voodoo gods, and discovered that zombies were real. While all this was going on, she knocked out the manuscript of the book that would make her nationally famous—*Their Eyes Were Watching God*—in a period of seven weeks. "In her spare time," one is tempted to sarcastically remark.

In Haiti, Zora studied with a major voodoo priest, who instructed his chief priestess to teach her songs, dances, and various rituals. She was also allowed to watch him heal the sick and, in one case, she reported, raise the dead. She also became an initiate in the voodoo religion. In the course of all this, Zora became very ill with a "violent gastric disturbance," and was convinced that it was related to her involvement with the practice. She decided to return to New York, when she had recovered enough to be able to undertake the journey home. And at home, the critics were raving about her new book. Inasmuch as *Their Eyes Were Watching God* is a literary work, rather than an anthropological one, I will forego any analysis of it, except to say that it is highly autobiographical, the story of a young woman's journey of self-discovery. She is ultimately triumphant, successful in her struggle for self-realization and autonomy. Zora was subsequently listed in the new edition of *Who's Who in America*; Edna St. Vincent Millay sent her a congratulatory telegram.

Zora's autobiography, *Dust Tracks on a Road*, was published in 1942 to critical acclaim. She was again listed in *Who's Who*, as well as *Twentieth Century American Authors* and

*Current Biography*. The *Saturday Evening Post* commissioned two articles from her, and she was asked to do a piece for *Reader's Digest*. And yet slowly, things began to unravel. Six of her books eventually went out of print, and she couldn't get a publisher to take on her latest manuscripts. At the point that she was about to go broke—this in 1950—she took a job as a maid in an upscale suburb of Miami.

Zora died in 1960, in relative poverty. "Immediately following her death," writes Valerie Boyd, "Fate itself seemed determined to efface her memory." What happened was indeed peculiar. Her memory, and her work, somehow disappeared from public and professional view. She went from being a star, to being completely forgotten. And then, for whatever reason, Alice Walker went looking for her grave in 1973, in Fort Pierce, Florida, in an obscure location, and placed a marker on the grave she believed was Zora's: "Zora Neale Hurston - A Genius of the South." Two years later, she published an article about Zora in *Ms.* magazine, "In Search of Zora Neale Hurston." This got the ball rolling, as ZNH began to experience a posthumous revival. Her books were brought back into print; *Their Eyes Were Watching God* wound up on dozens of university syllabi. Between 1975 and 2010 she was the subject of more than 400 doctoral dissertations (undoubtedly many more between 2010 and 2025). In 1991, *Mule Bone*, the play she wrote with Langston Hughes, was produced on Broadway. Today, she is rightly regarded as one of America's outstanding literary figures. For our purposes, however, I don't hesitate to add that she was one of the greatest, and most daring, anthropologists who ever lived.

Was she a "bohemian"? To me, at least, she falls into the category of bohemian in the sense that Virginia Woolf's niece, Virginia Nicholson, defined it in her book *Among the Bohemians*: "There are people in the world," she writes, "who will not make compromises with life. Their faces are turned like sunflowers towards the source of light, and even when battered and broken they refuse to give in to old age, sorrow, loss, defeat."

This is who, and what, Zora Neale Hurston really was.

CHAPTER 8
===
## CLAUDE LÉVI-STRAUSS

Other societies are perhaps no better than our own; even if we are inclined to believe they are, we have no method at our disposal for proving it. However, by getting to know them better, we are enabled to detach ourselves from our own society. Not that our own society is peculiarly or absolutely bad. But it is the only one from which we have a duty to free ourselves.

—*Tristes Tropiques* (1955)

There are only a handful of intellectual giants in recent Western thought; Claude Lévi-Strauss was one of them.(1) He was the founder of a field known as structural anthropology, or more generally, structuralism, but his influence on a number of disciplines was enormous. Lévi-Strauss produced a series of famous books—*The Elementary Structures of Kinship, Structural Anthropology, Tristes Tropiques, The Savage Mind*, among others—and dedicated himself to rehabilitating so-called primitive thought. In a word, his ideas about myth collapsed the distinction between this thought and European high culture. The essential thrust of all his work, according to journalist and historian Sanche de Gramont, was that there was no such thing as a superior society. Certainly, primitive thinking was his most famous idea, that which he was known for. Primitive thought, he strove to demonstrate via ethnological analyses (of totemism, for example), was not inferior to our own; it was just different.

L-S reached the height of his profession. From 1950 to 1974 he was the head of the department of social and economic sciences at the École Pratique des Hautes Études, and from 1959 to 1982 Professor of Social Anthropology at the prestigious Collège de France. On the occasion of his 100th birthday, in 2008, France literally went nuts with celebrations: the man was France itself, with a capital F. The epitome of French culture, French brilliance—*sans égal*. He was suddenly regarded as a major diplomatic asset, and every French magazine had his photo on the front cover. President Sarkozy went to his apartment to wish him a happy birthday. He was, in a word, lionized through the roof.

Before we can assess his achievement, however, it will be necessary to say a few words about structuralism. Basically, it's a methodology, a mode of analysis that focuses on the relationships among elements in a conceptual system. Structuralism has a Platonic flavor to it, as in the Parable of the Cave in *The Republic*: it seeks the "true reality," the light behind the shadows, the patterns that underlie the surface appearances. So for example, the anthropologist will live with some exotic culture and study its modes of food preparation, religious rites, games, kinship arrangements, mythologies, and so on, but with the goal of discovering the underlying structures that connects all of these things. These structures, according to L-S, formed the "deep grammar" (shades of Noam Chomsky) of that society. These originated in the mind and operated on an unconscious level.

The essence of structuralism, according to historian and editor Thomas Meaney, is to shift from the study of single objects (food preparation, etc.) to the study of the relationships among those objects. This form of investigation supposedly revealed the universals that could be found across all cultures and all times. "Within this project," writes the anthropologist Albert Doja, "the aim of structural anthropology is to arrive at structures so general as to be common to all societies, absolute to the extent they are universal categories of the human mind, that is, structural invariants organized in systems of significances." As L-S wrote in *Structural Anthropology*,

> If, as we believe to be the case, the unconscious activity of the mind consists in imposing forms upon content and if these forms are fundamentally the same for all minds, ancient and modern, primitive and civilized, it is necessary and sufficient to grasp the unconscious structure underlying each institution and each custom, in order to obtain a principle of interpretation valid for other institutions and other customs.

"How are we to explain the fact," he asked in the same text, "that myths throughout the world are so similar?" These structures are ahistorical, even a-cultural, since, as he says, they "are fundamentally the same for all minds, ancient and modern, primitive and civilized." In addition, myths operated in people's minds without their being aware of it, and he claimed (in the fourth and final volume of *Mythologiques*) that all the myths of the Americas constituted a single myth, one that has been told and retold for thousands of years.

All of this led L-S to be deeply critical of Western society and culture. He regarded the latter as an "unhealthy aberration" on a world scale. The savage mind, he asserted (Meaney again), "proposed remedies for specifically Western maladies." Certain native societies, he went on to say, had important things to teach us about how to integrate mankind into an intimate relationship with the world—something sorely lacking in the West. L-S denounced our "mass civilization," our "monoculture," and occasionally expressed disgust with the West and "its own filth, thrown in the face of mankind." He was a pioneer in ecology before it became fashionable, and repeatedly expressed his antipathy toward the Western obsession with the goal of dominating nature, as opposed to appreciating its complexity. He would have had no disagreement with the famous remark of Sitting Bull's, "the love of possessions is a disease with them."

In any case, the lionization of L-S began, in academic circles at least, long before 2008. While L-S had very few students or disciples, structuralism became the next "hula hoop" among French intellectuals. "It came to have something of the momentum of a millennial movement," wrote anthropologist Adam Kuper, "and some of its adherents felt that they formed a secret society in a world of the blind. Conversion was not just a matter of accepting a new paradigm. It was, almost, a question of salvation." Structuralism got applied to psychology (Lacan, Piaget), political theory (Althusser), feminism (Assiter), economics (the Prebisch-Singer hypothesis), literary theory (Barthes), and so on. It all calls to mind L-S' wry comment on cultured Parisian society, that "every five years or so, it needs to stuff something new in its mouth."

By implication, L-S may have offered a comment on civilization (Parisian society, for example) versus pre-civilization. The British author, Anthony Powell, believed that rosy pictures of the past were ahistorical and illusory, claiming that "freedom from one sort of humbug [his word for hula hoop] merely implying, with human beings of any epoch, thraldom to another." Like L-S, he was saying that we go from humbug to humbug, deceiving ourselves that we finally have The Answer every time. But L-S hardly believed that this analysis could be extended indefinitely into the past. After all, primitive society lasted for many millennia; it was not into hula-hooping, nor was it desperately seeking salvation. In terms of human life, it was hardly humbug. Just the opposite, in fact. (See the epigraph to this book.)(2)

And so we come to the ultimate question: Did Lévi-Strauss get it right? It's rather odd: if you check him out on the Internet, critiques of his *oeuvre* far outnumber the agreements with it, and his academic critics also outnumber his supporters. It turns out that while his achievement was extraordinary, there are, to my mind, too many snakes in this garden. Let me be explicit. (In what follows, I am merging my own criticisms with those of others.)

-L-S didn't do a great deal of actual fieldwork, at least in comparison with many other leading anthropologists. As Thomas Meaney writes, he was a "library man"—much like Lucien Lévy-Bruhl. For an anthropologist, this is rather problematic, and it shows up as a lack of empirical evidence just when such data are needed—for example, in his (metaphysical) claim that the mind contains a "deep grammar" that is the cause of everything. (How could one prove this?)

-In addition, as noted above, L-S claimed that myths operated in people's minds without their being aware of it. As Albert Doja points out, this claim is not grounded in any empirical reality, and taken to the extreme is a kind of ghost-in-the-machine theory of human cognition. Doja adds that he had "a single, quasi-demiurgic gift to flush out affinities of meaning from anywhere and anything." So some critics argue that he ignored history and geography, using myths from one place and time to supposedly illuminate myths from another place and time, without being able to demonstrate any genuine connection.

-Other critics argue that his focus on universal structures oversimplifies the complexity of various cultures, ignoring the nuances of daily life.

-He also dismisses the possibility of human agency, saying that the underlying structures of society "left little room" (Meaney, again) for it. His analysis is pretty deterministic; Sartre called it rigid and mechanical. In his *Critique of*

*Dialectical Reason*, he remarked "that Lévi-Strauss studied men the way entomologists study ants."(3)

-As in the case of Joseph Campbell, with his monomyth of the hero, L-S' study of myth might be accused of embodying a kind of Procrustean, one-size-fits-all approach. That, in other words, he was not so much finding things as imposing a prefabricated framework onto the data; "discovering" what he wanted to discover, in a word. Doja's remark, quoted above, that "the aim of structural anthropology is to arrive at structures so general as to be common to all societies," strikes me as being very Campbellian.

This affinity with Joseph Campbell, whom I regard as a pseudo-scholar of the first order, is the most disturbing possibility for me. There is just too much that L-S argues that is similar to Campbell's "it's all the same myth" approach. Campbell may have fooled American New Agers (even Bill Moyers and the poet Robert Bly, both of whom should have known better), but the criticisms of his work are both extensive and devastating: that his approach was one of flattening differences, and cherry-picking evidence; that he ignored the nuances and specifics of individual stories, and the diversity of thought that existed within different cultures; that he was simplistic and reductionistic. Franz Boas sharply criticized this type of approach in a lecture he gave at the 1896 meeting of the American Anthropological Association, saying that it was wrong-headed to believe that "the sameness of ethnological phenomena found in diverse regions is proof that the human mind obeys the same laws everywhere," adding that the burden of proof was on those who wish to argue "that there is one grand system according to which mankind has developed...." And in his essay on Campbell, Robert Segal (a professor of religious studies) shows how Campbell constructs a composite hero pattern and then takes things that don't conform to it as examples *of* it. Etc. Of course, L-S was hardly identical to Campbell, to say the least, but it seems to me that there is something of an overlap in methodology, which is just a trifle unsettling. All of which calls to mind a depressing old saw, that when myth meets fact, myth usually wins.(4)

So I leave Lévi-Strauss as a thinker with an ambiguous legacy. The celebration of his 100th birthday, referred to above, was not really about the content of his work, but rather about the man as a symbol of something; Frenchness, perhaps. His achievement, unlike that of Joseph Campbell's, was real, and his scholarly influence on so many fields, and so many thinkers, was considerable. But as to validating his theories: that would seem to be unresolved.

CHAPTER 9

# Marshall Sahlins

Free from market obsessions of scarcity, hunters' economic propensities may be more consistently predicated on abundance than our own.

—Marshall Sahlins, "The Original Affluent Society"

They are never in a hurry. Quite different from us, who can never do anything without hurry and worry...

—Pierre Biard, "Relation of New France, of Its Lands, Nature of the Country, and of Its Inhabitants"(1616)

[Sahlins] now stands as a sage among anthropologists, maybe the last one.

—Claude Lévi-Strauss

Marshall Sahlins (1930-2021) was a prolific author, having written nineteen books during his long career. But it is one particular book, *Stone Age Economics* (1972), for which he is especially remembered, inasmuch as, in a similar way to

Pierre Clastres and his call for a "Copernican revolution" (see below), he turned our perception of "primitive" societies upside-down. The book's influence went way beyond the boundaries of the academy. In the years following its publication, it captured the imagination of tens of thousands, young people especially. It remains, to this day, a deeply radical book, and as one anthropologist, Webb Keane, argued on the fiftieth anniversary of its publication, it stands up pretty well after all these years: "Today we can...find in his polemic against infinite needs and relentless consumption a genealogy of environmental destruction." Sahlin's work, he adds, constituted "a seismic transition in anthropological thought." He goes on to say:

> If the capitalist world seeks wealth through ever greater material production to meet infinitely expansive desires, foraging societies follow "the Zen road to affluence": not by getting more, but by wanting less. If it seems that foragers have been left behind by "progress," this is due only to the ethnocentric self-congratulation of the West. Rather than accumulate material goods, these societies are guided by other values: leisure, mobility, and above all, freedom.(1)

Sahlin's thesis does have a number of problems, and I'll be discussing these below. But for better or worse, the majority of anthropologists agree with Keane: Sahlins was onto something, and scholarship is much the better for it.

Sahlins did extensive fieldwork in the South Pacific, primarily Hawaii and Fiji. From 1957 to 1973 he was a professor at the University of Michigan, and then in 1973 was named Professor Emeritus of Anthropology at the University of Chicago. He was a heroic figure in many ways, famous for his political activism against US involvement in Vietnam, launching the teach-in movement that got picked up by many universities. Paralyzed, and literally on the verge of death, he completed his final work, *The New Science of the Enchanted Universe*, by dictating pages to his son, the historian Peter Sahlins. They finished the book a month before he died.(2)

Let's take a look at the famous essay, "The Original Affluent Society," which is the centerpiece of *Stone Age Economics*.(3) Of course, if you are going to try to persuade your readers that so-called primitive societies are rich, and that we moderns are poor—in effect, attempting to set fire to water—then you need to have at least three things going for you. One, Sahlins writes very well; his writing is clear and accessible, almost friendly. He draws the reader in. Two, he has a fair amount of empirical evidence to back up his thesis regarding the "affluence" of hunter-gatherers (HGs). And finally, he repeatedly characterizes our own economy as oppressive, a chasing after the infinite, with the typical individual caught in "a perpetual disparity between his unlimited wants and his insufficient means." All three of these elements serve to capture our attention, and reassure us that he has not left the planet.

It is also the case that his timing couldn't have been better. By 1966, there was widespread disenchantment with the Western, especially the American, way of life. Herbert Marcuse published *One-Dimensional Man* in 1964; the US deployed troops to Vietnam in 1965; and student activism was gaining momentum in the form of the anti-war movement, the civil rights movement, and the free-speech movement. Timothy Leary was dropping LSD, and Theodore Roszak (among others) was extolling the virtues of the counterculture. As all of this was swirling around, leading anthropologists mounted a "Man the Hunter" conference at the University of Chicago in 1966, and it was here that Sahlins first floated the idea of the original affluent society. An expanded version of his presentation was published two years later in Sartre's influential journal, *Les Temps modernes*—the same year of the May-June uprising in Paris. In a word, a great many people were open to the notion that modern life was not all it was cracked up to be, and that "there has to be a better way."

This search for a better way, moreover, would seem to be alive and well. As an aside, before reviewing Sahlin's essay, I need to point out the regular, and increasing, life stories that are posted on the Internet, of Americans who have left the US and report how much happier they are in their new, "relaxed" location. This has now become something of a drumbeat. In one recent case, a woman left California for Mazatlán, in Mexico, and her comments comparing Mexico and the US are quite typical, and also quite "Sahlinesque." "In the States," she says, "I always felt like I didn't have enough and I wasn't succeeding." Here in Mexico, "I don't worry when I go to Walmart that somebody's going to shoot me. I don't worry when I go to a street festival that someone's going to run a car through the people...I don't know how people live there [in the US]." Mexico is pretty much the opposite: "There's a heart here that is still beating," she declares. In fact, Woodrow Wilson knew the score as early as 1913: "The truth is, we are all caught in a great economic system which is heartless" (from his book *The New Freedom*). An early Sahlinite, we might say, although, of course, Marx beat him to the punch.(4)

As for Sahlin's essay: The conventional wisdom, which literally everyone believes, he tells us, is that HGs live pretty desperate lives, constantly scrambling to survive, in what is labeled a "subsistence economy." The truth is, that describes *us*, not them—his argument in a nutshell. Affluence, he goes on, can be achieved in two ways. The way of market economics is to pursue endless fulfillment, which is the life of a hamster on a wheel. "But there is also a Zen road to affluence, [which recognizes that] human material wants are finite and few...Adopting the Zen strategy, a people can enjoy an unparalleled material plenty—with a low standard of living." He goes on:

"Is it so paradoxical to contend that hunters have affluent economies...? Modern capitalist societies, however richly endowed, dedicate themselves to the proposition of scarcity. Inadequacy of economic means is the first principle of the world's wealthiest peoples." Again, it is a question of shifting our perspective 180 degrees. Here is how to not understand HG societies: "Having equipped the hunter with bourgeois impulses and paleolithic tools, we judge his situation hopeless in advance...We should [instead] entertain the empirical possibility that hunters are in business for their health, a finite objective, and that bow and arrow are adequate to that end."

"The empirical possibility..." Sahlins provides a lot of them. Sir George Grey's expeditions in the 1830s to western

Australia, for example, which reported that the natives were not "greatly pressed for want of food." More recently, there are the quantitative data collected by the American-Australian Scientific Expedition to Arnhem Land in 1948 (published in 1960). This includes information on hunting, plant collecting, food preparation, and weapon repair. What the data show is that the people in question don't work very hard: a total of four or five hours per person per day are invested in the appropriation and preparation of food. They also actually *underuse* their objective economic possibilities, and the mean daily consumption of calories was above 2,000. Sahlins comments:

> A good case can be made that hunters and gatherers work less than we do; and, rather than a continuous travail, the food quest is intermittent, leisure abundant, and there is a greater amount of sleep in the daytime per capita per year than in any other condition of society.

As for the Bushmen, specifically the Dobe section of the !Kung, Sahlins draws on the extensive fieldwork of Richard Lee, which indicates that their situation is the same as the HGs of Arnhem Land. Again, there is a lot of data to support his claim, which he discusses in detail. He then moves on to the Hadza tribe of Tanzania, and two or three other groups. "Clearly," he says in conclusion, "the hunting-gathering economy has to be revaluated." "There is nothing," he asserts, "...to the convention that hunters and gatherers can enjoy little leisure from the tasks of sheer survival." Finally, he throws down the gauntlet to the modern capitalist economy; sticks it to us, in a word:

> Above all, what about the world today? One-third to one-half of humanity are said to go to bed hungry every night. In the Old Stone Age the fraction must have been much smaller. *This* is the era of hunger unprecedented. Now, in the time of the greatest technical power, is starvation an institution...it was not until [modern] culture neared the height of its material achievements that it erected a shrine to the Unattainable: *Infinite Needs*.

Sahlins was not one to mince words. This is a stupid way to live, is what he is telling us. Not that we are going to escape from the hamster cage any time soon.

Marshall Sahlins was a remarkable thinker, powerful, daring, and immensely creative. Lévi-Strauss was right to call him a sage, it seems to me. But I don't want to let him off the hook too easily. Let's hear from his critics, before we move on. It is possible, says the anthropologist David Kaplan, that Professor Sahlins has given us a too-rosy picture of "the original affluent society."(5)

Kaplan begins by admitting that the "main features of this thesis now seem to be widely accepted by anthropologists," and that even with the various reservations that do exist, very few of them reject the central argument. Kaplan's response to this is to assert that this is the result of these folks supposedly being ideologically "seduced," caught up in "ideological yearnings." Given what I said above about the sixties' context of Sahlins' work, there is probably some truth to this, but as I'll discuss below, I think there are reasons to believe that his work cannot be so easily dismissed.

As for Kaplan's counter-evidence: here he is on more solid (empirical) ground. In the case of the Arnhem Land study cited by Sahlins, for example, it turns out that the data collected was done over a short period of time, but then extrapolated to a full seasonal cycle; which renders the argument questionable. The same problem shows up in the research done by Richard Lee with the Dobe section of the !Kung: "to buttress his argument concerning Bushmen well-being, Lee would like to extrapolate his findings from one portion of the seasonal cycle to the entire cycle, even though he is aware of the significant difference between the dry season and the wet season."

Then there is the problem of the definition of work. One obtains low figures for work time if it is framed in terms of hunting and gathering, but when you add in the time spent in processing food, making and repairing tools, housekeeping, the curing of skins, child care, and so on, the work time is much longer—as Lee himself admitted. Add to this are the problems of diet and nutrition. During the "Man the Hunter" conference, Lorna Marshall related that the "!Kung we worked with are very thin and... constantly expressed concern and anxiety about food." Nancy Howell, who spent two years among the Bushmen, affirmed that in her experience, they were very thin and frequently complained of hunger. Speaking of the !Kung, Melvin Konner comments (in *The Tangled Wing*) that to refer to a society with a 50 percent child mortality rate, and a life expectancy at birth of thirty years, as "affluent," is kind of strange.

Kaplan also calls into question Sahlins' thesis regarding limited wants, the "Zen economy." Among the !Kung, for example, there are persistent pressures to share what you have. This leads to a deliberate limitation on their work effort, since additional work means you have more, and this would result in pressures to share. To refuse to share is a no-no in tribal cultures; as one anthropologist noted, "people are very much aware that possessions give rise to envy and...they are fearful of the consequences of envy." Which calls into question the notion of limited wants as the basis of affluence.

All of this complicates the thesis of the original affluent society, and it is just as well that we modify it accordingly. When the dust settles, however, I don't find it surprising that most anthropologists remain in agreement with the central argument, and I don't think Kaplan's notion of "ideological seduction" can go very far as an explanation (although, as the British would say, it's not *totally* without merit). Meanwhile, what about *our* seduction? We need to consider the endless propaganda that surrounds us on a daily basis, broadcasting the notion that our lives are so much better than they were in previous times. We are literally soaking in this ideology of progress (or more accurately, "progress"), which is so pervasive that we don't realize that it's an ideology—one far more zealous and seductive than the one Kaplan is worried about. *New York Times* columnist Frank Rich called the American mythology machine "the greatest story ever sold." It really is the supreme snow job, at once brilliant and perverse. Meanwhile, propaganda notwithstanding, most of the citizens of modern industrial society experience their lives as oppressive, a rat race, the "daily grind." They live for weekends (TGIF), holidays, retirement, and call this "life." Rich's book, published twenty years ago, made no impact on the American people whatsoever, who continue to drown in the pablum of the American mythology.(6)

A paradigm example of the seductive nature of the modern ideology are the naïve, and in my opinion downright false, works of Steven Pinker, such as *The Better Angels of Our Nature* and *Enlightenment Now*. The latter book was pretty much reduced to ashes by the British philosopher John Gray, who pointed out that the "message of Pinker's book is that the Enlightenment produced all of the progress of the modern era and none of its crimes." An historian, Pinker is not. "To think of this book as any kind of scholarly exercise," Gray went on to say, "is a category mistake. The purpose of Pinker's laborious work is to reassure liberals that they are on 'the right side of history'." What we have is poor scholarship and a lopsided argument—an embarrassment, says Gray. Pinker comes off as a fool, a high-IQ moron, which can hardly be said of Marshall Sahlins. Not surprisingly, he has a large following, including Bill Gates, another non-historian, who has praised Pinker's work to the skies.(7)

Like Sahlins, let's not mince words: the West seems to be on its last legs, culturally, economically, politically, and especially, ecologically. HGs lasted for millennia; industrial society, after a very short period of time by comparison, would seem to be committing suicide. As Webb Keane pointed out, an economy based on infinite needs has landed us in the throes of a looming environmental disaster. Surely societies that endure must know something about how to live that we moderns lack. Richard Lee may have put it best:

> I am convinced that hunter-gatherer studies, far from being the fantasy of uncritical romantics, have a role to play...as part of a larger movement to recapture wholeness from an increasingly fragmented and alienating modernity.(8)

Amen, is all I can say, to that.

## Chapter 10

# Pierre Clastres

There is a form of powerfulness inherent in being able to live without power.

—Jae Jah Noh [Edwin Smith], *Do you see what I see?*

[I]t is as though these societies formed their political sphere in terms of an intuition...these societies astonish us by the subtlety with which they have posed and settled the question...They had a very early premonition that power's transcendence conceals a mortal risk for the group...Indian societies were able to create a means for neutralizing the virulence of political authority.

—Pierre Clastres, "Exchange and Power"

If it is less tiring to descend than it is to climb, is it not true, however, that thought is loyal to itself only when it moves against the incline?

—Pierre Clastres, "Copernicus and the Savages"

Pierre Clastres (1934-77) was, in the opinion of many, one of anthropology's greats. If you search for him online, you'll find that there are a number of critiques of his work, along the lines of his supposedly being a "romantic," but the overall opinion of his colleagues is very positive. With his fieldwork in South America during 1963-74, his study of how power operates in "primitive" cultures, and his bold speculations as to how the field of political anthropology needed to rethink its basic premises, he was truly a gift to that field.

Clastres was a student of Claude Lévi-Strauss' and Marshall Sahlins'. He was a director of research at the Centre National de la Recherche Scientifique (CNRS) during 1961-75. In 1975 he was appointed director of studies of religion and societies of South American indigenous peoples at the École Pratique des Hautes Études. His most famous work is a collection of essays published in 1974, *Society Against the State*. He would undoubtedly have published a lot more, but his life was tragically cut short at age forty-three, when he was killed in an auto accident.(1)

There is much to be said about Clastres, but as I indicated in the Introduction, my goal is to present cameos, and in this case, it means focusing on his singular contribution, the study of "primitive" societies and how they deal (or dealt) with the issue of power.(2) As for his database, this consisted of fieldwork among a number of Amerindian societies, including the Guayakí, the Guaraní, the Yanomami, and the Chulupi.(3) What was the result of this research? Essentially, that there was very little concentration of authority among these peoples. Power was not considered coercive, and the leaders, or chieftains, were in fact powerless. They had prestige, to be sure, but the system was monitored (if that's the right word) so as to prevent the leader from transforming his prestige into coercive power. To be specific, these societies possessed cultural mechanisms (also known as levelling mechanisms) designed to prevent the emergence of coercive power figures. Such societies were vastly different from the great Andean civilizations, let us say, or the Mexico (Tenochtitlan) of the Aztecs, in terms of how society was organized, and how power was manifested. In addition, Clastres was very critical of the conventional evolutionary view, which saw the State, or hierarchical societies in general, as being more developed than primitive ones; as being superior, in a word. Let me draw on some of the essays in *Society Against the State* to elaborate on these arguments.

One of my favorites in this collection is the first one, "Copernicus and the Savages." It's an intriguing title; what could Clastres have possibly meant by it? Let me switch from Poland to Russia for a moment, and Lenin's definition of politics: *kto kovo?*; that is to say, Who does what to whom? In typical social relations, writes Clastres, power is realized in the form of command/obedience; coercion, in short. But as he discovered, most of the Amerindian societies he studied and lived with were headed by leaders who did not possess any real power. There was no hierarchy, and no command/obedience relationship in force. "It is not evident to me," he tells us, "that coercion and subordination constitute the essence of political power *in all times and in all places.*" [Clastres' italics] We are, in short, faced with the riddle of powerless power.

Power, in other words, manifests itself in two modes, coercive and non-coercive. The former mode is simply a particular case; it is not the only model of true power. In the second essay, "Exchange and Power," he solves the riddle. "The most notable characteristic of the Indian chief consists of his almost complete lack of authority." What this individual is, according to the anthropologist Robert Lowie, is a "titular chief," and he is characterized by three essential traits:

1. He is a peacemaker, i.e., the tribe's moderating agency, settling disputes and smoothing things over when necessary.

2. He is generous with his possessions; he is required to give them away when asked. (Compare the remark of Sitting Bull's, previously quoted, that for white Americans, "the love of possessions is a disease with them.")

3. He is a good orator, an effective speaker. (In actuality, members of the tribe often pay no attention to him at all, so he is effectively blowing smoke.)

For many Amerindian societies, says Clastres, power exists "totally separate from violence and apart from any hierarchy." "Given their political organization, most [such societies] are distinguished by their sense of democracy and taste for equality." What we, as anthropologists, have been doing is looking at "primitive" societies and regarding them as powerless, and therefore inferior. But this lack of authority on the part of the chief, this "emptiness," is quite deceptive; a paradox, in fact. It is a function operating in a void. We might compare it to the open hand of karate, far more powerful than our own coercive version of power, which is an expression of force, as opposed to genuine strength. The truth is that we've got it all upside down. As a result, what is needed at this point, says Clastres, is a Copernican-style revolution, a "heliocentric conversion." Long overdue to leave Ptolemy behind.

But this raises an interesting question. Why did the State arise? Why did some people cease to be primitives? How did the figure of the despot arise? It couldn't have emerged from the chief, who has no real power, and thus couldn't prefigure the head of State. Some radical discontinuity must have occurred. Clastres addresses these questions in the final essay, which is also entitled "Society Against the State."

It turns out that one important modification must be made to the above picture. In wartime, the chief *does* have real power. It's the one exception to the general rule. After the war is over, things revert to status quo ante. But having had a taste of power, what if the chief likes it? What if he is seduced by it? What is ever-present, says Clastres, is the risk of an excessive desire on the part of the chief of going too far. If this happened, and instead of serving the tribe, he tried to get the tribe to serve him—well, that would be the origin of the State. But this move, Clastres maintains, never works. "Primitive society is such that *it does not permit the desire for prestige to be replaced by the will to power.*" [Italics Clastres'] Really? How does Clastres know this? Maybe, on occasion, it *does* work. And (for example) what if the tribe is unable to control such a development, which might constitute a slippery slope. What then?

Clastres is on firmer ground when he suggests that size, population pressure, might be a factor in the emergence of the State. There have been a number of demographic studies suggesting that this is the case. Clastres' own example is the villages of the Guaraní, which grew in size to several thousand. As a result, their chiefs did acquire some coercive power, even though it was not the product of war.

Clastres' third possibility is very suggestive, but—as far as I can make out—purely speculative. I'm referring to the emergence of charismatic prophets as leaders. The primitive chief typically engages in innocent (even boring) speech, but under certain conditions, the tribe can get caught up in prophetic (vatic) speech, the language of seers: "In the discourse of the prophets there may lie the seeds of discourse of power, and beneath the exalted features of the mover of men, the one who tells them of their desire, the silent figure of the Despot may be hiding." He could be right; we in the West have had no lack of gurus, whose hidden agenda is their own self-aggrandizement. Or to put it another way, the will to power is the curse of mankind.

How, then, to evaluate this remarkable scholar, who bade fair to turn his profession upside down? If the profession didn't follow his lead into a "heliocentric conversion," they nevertheless recognized that they were dealing with a genius, whose insights couldn't be easily dismissed. A few tried, of course, but they don't represent the majority opinion. Clifford Geertz, for example—whose own work never addressed the issue of power—weighed in against Clastres with a dismissive string of sarcasms: he was a "romantical pilgrim;" he was "examining a handful of battered and powerless left-luggage Indians"; his research was of the "close-in, dogged-does-it sort" (I have no idea what this means), and so on.(4) What is going on here was accurately pegged by another anthropologist, Augusto Gayubas: "[Clastres'] research work was abruptly interrupted in 1977 when a car accident ended his life, but his disruptive thinking and active personality keep him present as a ghost among those who make their best efforts to silence the political consequences of his work." It's not rocket science: Clastres frightened Geertz, so in lieu of mounting a serious scholarly critique, he attempted to discredit him, erase him from professional consideration. Happily, he failed.(5)

"Disruptive thinking...active personality"...Should we call Clastres a "bohemian," in the sense that I characterized Zora Neale Hurston (above)? He has been accused of being an anarchist, at least, which may not be entirely off the mark. And of course, that might be a *good* thing. Let's just state it plainly: Pierre Clastres was not merely a remarkable anthropologist; he is also one of the most courageous people in modern memory.

# Epilogue: Great Lives

And so we come to the end of our journey, the story of ten great thinkers who saw through time; who looked into other "exotic" societies, "primitive" ones, and saw that they held up a mirror to our own. "Civilization ain't what it usta be," we might say; or at least, it appears to be very different as a result of their research. Cultural relativism suggests that these societies might be healthier than our own.

What are we left with, then, in the modern world? Have a look: a popular American actress, Sydney Sweeney, is marketing soap infused with her bathwater. According to an online post, "Sydney's Bathwater Bliss" soap bars can now be yours. A best-seller, for sure.

And then there are Gwyneth Paltrow's candles, which (she exclaims with delight) smell like her vagina, available for $75 a pop, and which sold out overnight. They constitute "a feminist statement," she says, although exactly what that statement consists of is rather obscure. This is the focus of millions of Americans; their lives are filled with this sort of

## Epilogue: Great Lives

consumerist nonsense, which includes the Mercedes Benz Janis Joplin sang about (ironically) many years ago. And all the while, slaughter and starvation continue in Palestine, while the rest of the world just looks on and does nothing. Add to which, the slaughters in the Ukraine and elsewhere. Welcome to the modern "civilized" world. Who, really, are the savages? Western neoliberals, with their world of war and genocide and hustling and competition and plutocracy and endless desire to show off (and the wokes, with their tiresome virtue-signaling), or the *indígenas*, with their inherent modesty, and their kinship worldview? Yes, I know this dichotomy is a bit too stark, and needs nuance and modification; but as a "first vintage," in the words of Francis Bacon, it is hardly off-base. Recall the poem by Ernest Hopkins, cited in the chapter on Alfred Kroeber, with his comment on Ishi: "What if you've got it on us?"; What if it is *your* way of life that is superior? A rhetorical question, one might argue. To my mind, for what it's worth, I regard modern society as shabby, tawdry, and incredibly stupid; destructive and self-destructive beyond belief. Barbara Ehrenreich once labeled it "psychotic." Was she being extreme, or was this spot-on?

Hegel wrote that history was a "slaughter bench." But native cultures, as Pierre Clastres points out, live outside of history, not in linear, "progressive" time. Hence the attempt of our ten anthropologists, among others, to find something better than the world of vagina candles, Holocausts, and the zealous butchery of Gaza. Of course, they didn't succeed, except theoretically; Clastres, for example, had a significant impact on the field of anthropology—praise of his work can be found all over the Internet—but his "heliocentric conversion" never really took hold, and certainly not in the public mind. Critics of (most of) the anthropologists profiled in this book attack their vision as "romantic," but I think the eminent sociologist, C. Wright Mills, had it right when he labeled this criticism "crackpot realism." What Mills was saying is that we've got the world upside down; our priorities are completely inverted. We don't have our heads pasted on straight. Gregory Bateson, for example, spent his whole professional life arguing this.

It would seem that the horror, the frivolity, and the dysfunctionality of the modern era just has to play itself out. Maybe then, when it hits a brick wall and starts to crack up—a tectonic shift already in progress, it seems to me—will alternatives such as the kinship worldview, with its attendant values of community, cooperation, craftsmanship, and sustainability, start to capture our attention. (Please God, it won't be too hermetic, or crammed full of trendy buzzwords.) This does not mean returning to a primitive state, which is not possible, and would not be desirable in any case. But it does mean trying to recapture *elements* of that way of life, ones that are profoundly human. (How to do that, of course, remains an open question.) To varying degrees, this is what our anthropologists were fighting for. It may be humanity's only hope.

As for me, this book is my own attempt, no matter how limited, how minuscule, to set things right-side up again; to throw my lot in with the alternatives as best as I know how. Thank you for listening, my friends; your willingness to consider these issues means a lot to me.

# Notes

*Introduction*

1. Arthur Koestler, *The Sleepwalkers* (New York: Penguin, 2014; orig. publ. 1959). On Bolsen, see various talks available on YouTube.

2. In the discussion that follows I am drawing on Appendix III of my book *Neurotic Beauty* (Healdsburg CA: Water Street Press, 2015).

*Chapter 1*

1. This and the following discussion are based on the following sources: "Lucien Lévy-Bruhl," in the *Encyclopaedia Herder* and the *New World Encyclopedia*; S.A. Mousalimas, "The Concept of Participation in Lévy-Bruhl's 'Primitive Mentality'," *Journal of the Anthropological Society of Oxford*, vol. 21 no. 1 (1990), pp. 33-46; and Jean

Cazeneuve, *Lucien Lévy-Bruhl*, trans. Peter Rivière (New York: Harper & Row, 1972).

2. Richard Shweder, "Anthropology's romantic rebellion against the enlightenment, or there's more to thinking than reason and evidence," in R.A. Shweder and R.A. LeVine (eds.), *Culture Theory: Essays on Mind, Self, and Emotion* (New York: Cambridge University Press, 1984). Note that a lot of mystical participation involves action-at-a-distance, the basis of Newton's Law of Universal Gravitation, and hence, of modern science.

3. Morris Berman, *The Soul of Russia* (Brattleboro VT: Echo Point Books & Media, 2023).

*Chapter 2*

1. The following discussion is based on Noga Arikha, *Franz Boas: In Praise of Open Minds* (New Haven: Yale University Press, 2025); Sol Tax, "Franz Boas," at britannica.com; Arturo Álvarez Roldán, "Franz Boas and the Concept of Culture," at https://teoriaehistoriaantropologia.blogspot.com/2012/04/boas-y-el-concepto-de-cultura.html; Thomas Hylland Eriksen and Finn Sivert Nielsen, *A History of Anthropology* (2d ed.; London: Pluto Press, 2013); Douglas Cazaux Sackman, *Wild Men* (New York: Oxford University Press, 2010); Louis Menand, "The Looking Glass," *New Yorker*, 26 August 2019; Charles King, *Gods of the Upper Air* (New York: Vintage, 2020); and "Franz Boas," Wikipedia.

## Chapter 3

1. This and the discussion that follows are based on the following sources: from Wikipedia, "Alfred Kroeber" and "Ishi in Two Worlds"; film, *The Last of His Tribe*, dir. Harry Hook, 1992; Jack Glazier, "The Kroeber-Ishi Story : Three Cinematic Versions," *Encyclopédie Bérose des histoires de l'anthropologie*, 2022; Douglas Cazaux Sackman, *Wild Men* (New York: Oxford University Press, 2010); and Theodora Kroeber, *Ishi in Two Worlds* (Berkeley: University of California Press, 1961).

## Chapter 4

1. Sources for this chapter include Margaret Caffrey, *Ruth Benedict* (Austin: University of Texas Press, 1989); Morris Berman, *Neurotic Beauty: An Outsider Looks at Japan* (Healdsburg CA: Water Street Press, 2015); Thomas Hylland Eriksen and Finn Sivert Nielsen, *A History of Anthropology* (2d ed.; London: Pluto Press, 2013); Ruth Benedict, *Patterns of Culture* (Boston: Mariner Books Classics, 2006; orig. publ. 1934), and *The Chrysanthemum and the Sword* (Boston: Mariner Books Classics, 2006; orig. publ. 1946); "Ruth Benedict," Wikipedia; "Ruth Benedict," at https://www.britannica.com/biography/Ruth-Benedict; Peter Crawford, "Patterns of Culture by Ruth Benedict," at https://www.ebsco.com/research-starters/literature-and-writing/patterns-culture-ruth-benedict; "'Patterns of Culture (1934)' by Ruth Benedict," at https://www.observingthemortals.com/index.php/2024/08/16/patterns-of-culture-1934-by-ruth-benedict; "Ruth Benedict," at Patterns of Culture Summary and Study Guide|Super Summary;

and "Culture and Personality Approach," at https://sociopedia.co/post/culture-and-personality-school; Jane Howard, *Margaret Mead* (New York: Fawcett Columbine, 1984); Benjamin Breen, *Tripping on Utopia* (New York: Grand Central Publishing, 2024); Lois Banner, *Intertwined Lives* (New York: Knopf, 2003); Louis Menand, "The Looking Glass," *New Yorker*, 26 August 2019; and Charles King, *Gods of the Upper Air* (New York: Vintage, 2020).

2.The classic study of romantic love in the West is Denis de Rougemont, *Love in the Western World*, trans. Montgomery Belgion (New York: Pantheon, 1956; orig. French ed. 1939).

3.See citations of King and Menand in n.1. King believes that the anthropologists arguing for cultural relativism changed people's attitudes and behaviors; that racism, gender bias, homophobia, and antagonism to the "Other," for example, have significantly decreased. In reviewing this, Menand asserts, *au contraire*, that all of these things are still very much with us. I'm inclined to think he's right, even if some modifications have taken place over the last few decades.

*Chapter 5*

1.The literature on Margaret Mead is colossal; here are just a few of my sources. Margaret Caffrey, *Ruth Benedict* (Austin: University of Texas Press, 1989); Jane Howard, *Margaret Mead* (New York: Fawcett Columbine, 1984); Thomas Hylland Eriksen and Finn Sivert Nielsen, *A History of Anthropology* (2d ed.; London: Pluto Press, 2013); "Margaret Mead," Wikipedia; Thomas Hylland Eriksen, Review of *Euphoria*, by Lily King, at https://www.hyllan

deriksen.net/blog/2018/12/13/sex-and-temperament-mead-bateson-and-fortune-new-guinea-1933; Mary Catherine Bateson, *With a Daughter's Eye* (New York: Harper Perennial, 2001; orig. ed. 1984); "Culture and Personality Approach," at https://sociopedia.co/post/culture-and-personality-school; Sam Dresser, "The meaning of Margaret Mead," at https//aeon.co/essays/how-margaret/mead-became-a-hate-figure-for-conservatives, 21 January 2020; Lois Banner, *Intertwined Lives* (New York: Knopf, 2003); Benjamin Breen, *Tripping on Utopia* (New York: Grand Central Publishing, 2024); "Margaret Mead," at Margaret Mead | Biography, Contributions, Books, Anthropology, & Oceania | Britannica; Charles King, *Gods of the Upper Air* (New York: Vintage, 2020); Louis Menand, "The Looking Glass," *New Yorker*, 26 August 2019; Derek Freeman, *Margaret Mead and Samoa: The Making and Unmaking of an Anthropological Myth* (Cambridge: Harvard University Press, 1983), and *The Fateful Hoaxing of Margaret Mead* (New York: Basic Books, 1998); "Derek Freeman," Wikipedia; and Paul Shankman, *The Trashing of Margaret Mead* (Madison: University of Wisconsin Press, 2009). Regarding the impact of Mead, and the cultural relativists in general, see above, Chapter 4, n.3, along with the discussion at the end of that chapter.

## Chapter 6

1. On the following discussion see Gregory Bateson, *Steps to an Ecology of Mind* (Frogmore, St. Albans, Herts.: Paladin, 1973); *Naven* (2d ed.; Stanford: Stanford University Press, 1958); *Mind and Nature* (New York: Dutton, 1979); "Men Are Grass: Metaphor and the World of Mental Process"

(Lindisfarne Association, pamphlet, 1980); John Brockman (ed.), *About Bateson* (New York: Dutton, 1977); Morris Berman, *The Reenchantment of the World* (2d ed.; Ithaca: Cornell University Press, 1983); Brian Stagoll, "Gregory Bateson at 100," *Australian and New Zealand Journal of Family Therapy*, vol. 27 no. 3 (2006), pp. 121-34; "Gregory Bateson," Wikipedia; Thomas Hylland Eriksen, Review of *Euphoria*, by Lily King, at www.hyllanderiksen.net/blog/2018/12/13/sex-and-temperament-mead-bateson-and-fortune-new-guinea-1933; Thomas Hylland Eriksen and Finn Sivert Nielsen, *A History of Anthropology* (2d ed.; London: Pluto Press, 2013); Jane Howard, *Margaret Mead* (New York: Fawcett Columbine, 1984); Peter Harries-Jones, "'From Anthropology to Epistemology': Extensions to an Autobiography of Gregory Bateson," *Encyclopédie Bérose des histoires de l'anthropologie*, 2021; Mary Catherine Bateson, *With a Daughter's Eye* (New York: Harper Perennial, 2001; orig. ed. 1984); Benjamin Breen, *Tripping on Utopia* (New York: Grand Central Publishing, 2024); and David Lipset, *Gregory Bateson: The Legacy of a Scientist* (Boston: Beacon Press, 1982).

2. See citation of Stagoll in n.1.

3. The exact title of the article is "The Specific Laws of Logic in Schizophrenia," by E. von Domarus, in Jacob Kasanin (ed.), *Language and Thought in Schizophrenia* (Los Angeles and Berkeley: University of California Press, 1944).

4. Bateson would seem to be saying something similar to the argument of Benedict, Kroeber, and Pirsig about the validity of subjective truth, briefly discussed in Chapter 4, above. See discussion below, regarding William Bateson's

philosophical outlook. Brian Stagoll comments on this (see citation in n.1, above): "His preference for thinking in aesthetic terms, of pattern rather than quantitative and reductive terms, provides an alternative to the dominant and (to Bateson) pathological systems of thought afflicting industrial civilization."

5.In the discussion that follows I am drawing on *The Reenchantment of the World*, the work of David Lipset, and that of Mary Catherine Bateson, all cited in n.1 above.

6.William Coleman, "Bateson and Chromosomes: Conservative Thought in Science," *Centaurus*, Vol. 15, Issue 3 (December 1971), pp. 228-314.

7.For a comprehensive discussion of the degrowth movement see Degrowth - Wikipedia.

8.I did my best to explicate GB's work in *The Reenchantment of the World*, but I would also recommend the detailed analysis provided by Peter Harries-Jones in the article cited in n.1, and also the following books on Bateson by the same author: *A Recursive Vision* (1995) and *Upside-Down Gods* (2016), in addition to the biography of GB by David Lipset, also cited in n.1. Quotes from Stagoll: see citation in n.1. Blake's "Newton" hangs in the Tate Britain; his poem was contained in a letter to Thomas Butts, 22 November 1802.

9.Wallerstein died in 2019. A Google search for him generates numerous biographical profiles, and a partial list of his publications can be found at amazon.com. For our own purposes, I would recommend *Utopistics* (New York: New Press, 1998).

10.Bateson never referred to the Surrealist movement in his work, but there is some scholarly discussion as to whether it genuinely constitutes an alternative epistemology to Western empirical science. It does strike me as also being inchoate, or tentative—a job half-done, a groping toward a possibility (which is not to necessarily discredit it). See, for example, Elizabeth Hamilton, "Surpassing realism: How surrealism offers an alternative," at therattlecap.com, 29 February 2024.

*Chapter 7*

1.On the following see Valerie Boyd, *Wrapped in Rainbows* (New York: Scribner, 2003); in Wikipedia: "Zora Neale Hurston," "Harlem Renaissance," "Hoodoo (spirituality)," and *"Their Eyes Were Watching God"*; Fenton Johnson, *At the Center of All Beauty* (New York: Norton, 2020); Louis Menand, "The Looking Glass," *New Yorker*, 26 August 2019, and "Why Zora Neale Hurston Was Obsessed with the Jews," *New Yorker*, 13 January 2025; "Life Story: Zora Neale Hurston (1891–1960)," at Life Story: Zora Neale Hurston (1891–1960) - Women & the American Story; Alisha R. Norwood, "Zora Neale Hurston," at Zora Neale Hurston, 2017; Cheryl Dowe Carpenter, "Zora Neale Hurston," at Zora Neale Hurston - Encyclopedia of Alabama, 21 April 2008 and 13 October 2023; and Alice Walker, "In Search of Zora Neale Hurston," at Walker_In_Search_of_Zora.pdf.

*Chapter 8*

1.This discussion of Lévi-Strauss is based on the following sources: From Wikipedia: "Structuralism" and "Claude

Lévi-Strauss"; Thomas Meaney, "Library Man: On Claude Lévi-Strauss," *The Nation*, 19 January 2011 (This is a review of a biography of Lévi-Strauss by Patrick Wilcken, *Claude Lévi-Strauss: The Poet in the Laboratory.*); Greg Downey, "Thinking through Claude Lévi-Strauss," at Thinking through Claude Lévi-Strauss – Neuroanthropology, 8 November 2009; James J. Fox, "Claude Lévi-Strauss," at Memoirs_18-14-Levi-Strauss.pdf; Maurice Bloch, Lévi-Strauss obituary, *The Guardian*, 3 November 2009; Edward Rothstein, "Claude Lévi-Strauss Dies at 100," *New York Times*, 4 November 2009; Sanche de Gramont, "There Are No Superior Societies," *New York Times Magazine*, 28 January 1968; Albert Doja, "The shoulders of our giants: Claude Lévi-Strauss and his legacy in current anthropology," *Social Science Information*, 2006, 45 (1), pp.79-107; Joel Christensen and Sarah Bond, "The Man Behind the Myth: Should We Question the Hero's Journey?", *Los Angeles Review of Books*, 12 August 2021; and Morris Berman, "The Hula Hoop Theory of History," Counterpunch, 11 January 2013.

2.Anthony Powell, *A Dance to the Music of Time*, vol. 9: *The Military Philosophers*, p. 227.

3.As quoted by Sanche de Gramont; see citation in n.1.

4.Cf. Jane Harrison, *Prolegomena to the Study of Greek Religion* (3d ed.; Meridian Books, 1955), p. 380: "anthropologists are slow to face solid historical fact." See Franz Boas, "The Limitations of the Comparative Method of Anthropology," *Science*, n.s., vol. 4 no. 103 (18 December 1896), pp. 901-8, and Robert Segal, "Joseph Campbell's Theory of Myth," in Alan Dundes (ed.), *Sacred Narrative*

(Berkeley: University of California Press, 1984), pp. 256-57 and 263-68. This is not the place to provide an extended critique and dissection of Campbell's work, but for readers who might be interested, see my *Wandering God* (Albany: SUNY Press, 2000), Chapter 1, n. 6, and Chapter 4, nn. 2 and 14.

*Chapter 9*

1.Marshall Sahlins, *Stone Age Economics* (New York: Aldine de Gruyter, 1972); Webb Keane, "Marshall Sahlins's 'Original Affluent Society' 50 Years Later," at Marshall Sahlins's "Original Affluent Society" 50 Years Later - Public Books. Not surprisingly, Pierre Clastres wrote the preface to the French edition of *Stone Age Economics*.

2.Ellen Ferry and Naomi Blumberg, "Marshall Sahlins," at britannica.com; "Marshall Sahlins," Wikipedia.

3.The essay can be downloaded from several sites online, e.g., from the University of Vermont, among others: Sahlins-Original_Affluent_Society.pdf.

4.Tamara Hardingham-Gill, "'I always felt like I didn't have enough': Why this American woman moved from California to Mexico 20 years ago | CNN," 4 June 2025.

5.David Kaplan, "The Darker Side of the 'Original Affluent Society'," *Journal of Anthropological Research*, vol. 56, no. 3 (Autumn, 2000), pp. 301-324. To my knowledge, Sahlins never replied to this essay.

6.Frank Rich, *The Greatest Story Ever Sold* (New York: Penguin, 2006).

NOTES

7.John Gray, "Unenlightened thinking: Steven Pinker's embarrassing new book is a feeble sermon for rattled liberals," *New Statesman*, 22 February 2018. As a side note, it is even more embarrassing that Pinker appeared on a racist, right-wing podcast known as Aporia. The Guardian (7 June 2025) reported on this as follows: "Patrik Hermansson, a researcher at UK anti-racism non-profit Hope Not Hate, said that Pinker's 'decision to appear on Aporia, a far-right platform for scientific racism, provides an invaluable service to an extremist outlet by legitimising its content and attracting new followers...By lending his Harvard credentials to Aporia, Pinker contributes to the normalisation and spread of dangerous, discredited ideas'." Pinker avoided all attempts to contact him. See Harvard author Steven Pinker appears on podcast linked to scientific racism | Steven Pinker | The Guardian. As for the adulation of Bill Gates, there are several articles reporting on this, for example, Philip Galanes, "The Mind Meld of Bill Gates and Steven Pinker," *New York Times*, 27 January 2018.

8.Lee quoted in Kaplan, "The Darker Side..."

*Chapter 10*

1."Pierre Clastres," Wikipedia.

2.Sources for the following discussion include the profile in Wikipedia and *Society Against the State*, trans. Robert Hurley and Abe Stein (New York: Zone Books, 1989; orig. French ed. 1974).

3. Interestingly enough, Clastres' *Chronicle of the Guayaki Indians* was translated by the eminent American author, Paul Auster, who declared that he loved the book. For negative reviews of it, and assertions of Clastres' "romanticism," see Clifford Geertz, "Deep Hanging Out," *New York Review of Books*, 22 October 1998, and Bartholemew Dean, "Critical Re-Vision: Clastres' Chronicle and the Optic of Primitivism," *Anthropology Today*, vol. 15 no. 2 (April 1999). See also Samuel Moyn, "Of Savagery and Civil Society: Pierre Clastres and the Transformation of French Political Thought," *Modern Intellectual History*, vol. 1 (2004), pp. 55-80.

4. See Geertz citation in n.3.

5. Augusto Gayubas, "Pierre Clastres and societies against the State," *Germinal. Journal of Libertarian Studies*, no. 9 (January-June 2012); reprinted at acracia.org. For a responsible (if rather brief) critique of Clastres' work, see John Gledhill, *Power and Its Disguises* (London: Pluto Press, 1994), pp. 32 and 39-40.

# About the Author

Morris Berman is a poet, novelist, essayist, social critic, and cultural historian. He has written twenty-eight books and nearly 200 articles, and has taught at a number of universities in Europe, North America, Chile, and Mexico. He won the Governor's Writers Award for Washington State in 1990, and was the first recipient of the annual Rollo May Center Grant for Humanistic Studies in 1992. In 2000, *The Twilight of American Culture* was named a "Notable Book" by the *New York Times Book Review*, and in 2013 he received the Neil Postman Award for Career Achievement in Public Intellectual Activity from the Media Ecology Association. Dr. Berman lives in Mexico.

Printed in Dunstable, United Kingdom